To pro John Gray

from Dmitri
Shlapentokh

The Proto-Totalitarian STATE

The Proto-Totalitarian STATE

Punishment and Control
in Absolutist Regimes

Dmitry Shlapentokh

Transaction Publishers
New Brunswick (U.S.A.) and London (U.K.)

Library of Congress Catalog Number: 2007002212
ISBN: 978-0-7658-0366-5
Printed in the United States of America

Library of Congress Cataloging-in-Publication Data

Shlapentokh, Dmitry.
    The Proto-totalitarian state / Dmitry Shlapentokh.
        p. cm.
    Includes bibliographical references and index.
    ISBN-13: 978-0-7658-0366-5
    1. Totalitarianism. 2. state, The. I. Title.

JC480.S56   2006
321.9—dc22   2007002212

Contents

Introduction

The major goal of our work is to prove that in some cases brutal totalitarian regimes, or at least regimes with significant totalitarian attributes, have been the only way to maintain basic social order. Moreover, we intend to show that these totalitarian or semi-totalitarian regimes (those with attributes of a totalitarian society) were not the product of "discourse," a wrong ideology that somehow took over the elite and the rest of society as well. Although ideology played an important role in many totalitarian regimes, it was hardly the chief reason for the existence of controlling or repressive systems. Maintaining basic order is one of the most important, if not the most important, tasks of the elite in all societies; the interaction between the elite and the rest of society and the elite's response to the needs of society are the most important variables. For example, in fourteenth- through sixteenth-century France, when the general meltdown of the entire society was based on asocial behavior that affected all groups and all aspects of their interactions—from social to sexual to the way people disposed of their waste. In this situation, the state, engaging in "normalizing" society, confronted the entire society and acquired distinctly totalitarian features in the process.

This work will argue that this essential aspect of the activities of totalitarian or semi-totalitarian states has been obscured in modern thought, especially Anglo-American thought, which almost always takes for granted that the majority are part of this or that social group and that asocial behaviors are the actions of a few marginalized individuals. This is the reason why many social scientists reduce the rise of modern totalitarian regimes to the influence of "wrong" ideologies. I will argue that not ideology but social conditions led to the rise of totalitarian governments and that the interaction between these states and society must be examined closely. The interaction must not be perceived in the traditional Marxist sense. For Marx, the state, while employing violence (in fact, he saw violence as an essential aspect of the state), did so mostly in the name of the ruling class; in effect, he saw the state as the tool of the ruling elite.

This approach is challenged here. Totalitarian and semi-totalitarian states confronted not only the lower classes, but all socioeconomic levels of the societies they ruled. This was done not because of the "discursive" drive for power, ideological obsessions, the internal logic of the development of the state apparatus, or even the need to mobilize state resources for foreign adventures, although all these variables must be taken into account, but because the society could not hold together on its own.

A certain amount of control and repressiveness is essential for the functioning of all societies, but it is especially crucial during certain periods of history, in certain places. At times a strong government with an assortment of repressive measures is the only way a society can survive. But why is the importance of the need for the state to take repressive/controlling actions marginalized or ignored in social science? Why is ideology/culture, lust for power and material benefits of power, or drive for imperial aggrandizement often given as the explanatory model of authoritarian/totalitarian governments?

The major reason, of course, is that Western societies are not in danger of being overwhelmed by criminalized anarchy, cases of criminal behavior notwithstanding. Thus, the importance of the asocial process in shaping the historical process was already lost sight of by the nineteenth century. Nineteenth-century sociology would downplay the role of asocial processes in the social process. Although sociologists would elaborate on conflicts, in almost all cases they detailed the conflicts as between various social, political, and ethnic groups or between the state and these groups. Nineteenth-century sociology would basically ignore conflicts between the state, which in some cases stayed outside the social interplay, and its criminal elements—the society of anomies. Moreover, the notion of society as an aggregation of anomies would be seen as a contradiction in terms.

Indeed, the notion of society implied the cohesiveness of various groups. In this arrangement, asocial elements and processes (elements that would be in opposition to the entire society) would be marginalized. This would especially be the case with Anglo-Saxon sociological traditions, which took as axiomatic the notion that each individual, with few exceptions, was attached to one group or another. These notions would come to dominate twentieth-century sociology, especially American sociology.

Thus, the major reason for modern sociology to ignore or marginalize the role of asocial processes (necessitating a strong/repressive government) in shaping major historical events is the fact that these conditions (situations where criminality threatened the very existence of the society) have not been part of the historical picture in the West for centuries.

Consequently, modern social scientists generally fail to understand the role of controlling/repressive elements and the importance of order, in the holistic meaning of the word, for society. Order and a strong repressive aspect of the society/state are mostly seen as caused by the desires of the elite to maintain power or as a product of ideological drives; this last explanation is most important in our case.

Indeed, while there are many explanations of the emergence of the modern totalitarian society, the most popular is that its rise is due to the spread of certain ideologies. This notion developed in the course of post-World War II history and obscured many other roles of totalitarian regimes, including their repressive policies as being the only way to maintain basic order. Due to the importance of this notion and its spell over many explanatory models of totalitarian regimes, it is critical to see how it emerged and changed. At the same time, we shall look beyond the discursive model to see the real causes of the rise of repressive/controlling aspects of totalitarian regimes, for it is clear that no one theory can explain the rise of all totalitarian regimes.

Thus, the goal of this book can be condensed to the following. It is most important to discard the notion of the totalitarian system as "discourse," a concept that has dominated intellectual thought. Most pundits have visualized the totalitarian regime as the product of an ideology that the ruling elite imposed upon the helpless society. These visions of the regimes ignore their essential roles in the development of society, for example, the totalitarian state's role in economic development or upgrading the military potential of the country. These essential roles are either discarded or marginalized. It also goes without saying the vision of the totalitarian state as the product of an artificial quasi-religious ideology provides no room for the role of these regimes in maintaining basic order. In fact, the assumption that at times a repressive government is essential for the maintenance of basic order was rejected not only by the conservatives who rallied against the Soviet and Chinese totalitarian regimes, but also by the liberals and the Left, who often discarded the term of "totalitarian regime" itself.

In their view, repressive external control is absolutely not needed, and the citizens, upon being liberated from the controlling and repressive power of totalitarian regimes, can easily control their asocial drives. It was assumed in this context that asocial drives are marginal, for the great majority of the people are part of this or that self-policed cohesive social group. Basic order and security are a given.

Only recently has the situation started to change. Russian intellectuals have been in the vanguard. Many of them were horrified by the criminal anarchy that overwhelmed post-Soviet Russia, and some started to look favorably toward the time of the repressive Soviet regime, which is beginning to be appreciated for its stability and comparative security. In this vision, the asocial drives that grip post-Soviet Russia today are seen as more dangerous than the repression during the Soviet era.

Of course, the views of these Russian intellectuals were marginalized and dismissed as a manifestation of their reactionary ideology, not only in Russia but also outside its borders. Their view was thought of as absolutely irrelevant to the West in general and the U.S. in particular. Yet the situation has started to change since September 11, 2001 and the events that have unfolded afterward. For first time in history, Americans fear for their personal safety, a fear shared by all segments of society.

The asocial elements of society (criminals), or those who can be seen as structurally similar to them (terrorists), have ceased to be a "discourse"—the product of the intellectual interplay and arbitrary labeling of the ruling elite. Asocial groups, and the processes directly or indirectly connected with them, have become a real threat that has spilled into the international arena, supplanting the fear of a nuclear Armageddon with the USSR. There are various manifestations of this fear. There is the fear of the spread of weapons of mass destruction among terrorists and "rogue" states. The chaos that emerged after the collapse of Saddam Hussein's regime in Baghdad and American inability to stop it have implied that similar events are possible globally. This has created the sense that a strong state is necessary to maintain stability both inside and outside international borders.

Although the threat to personal safety and the fear of anarchy in the broad sense have not entirely changed the view of repressive regimes, at least there is a visible new trend. Fear has challenged the assumption that asocial behavior and processes related to it are merely "discourse," for instance, the notion that calling terrorists "terrorists" is merely the manifestation of "hegemonic discourse." Conservative intellectuals continue to see the roots of terrorism in "wrong" ideologies, in this case the spread of fundamentalist Islam, but some of their other basic assumptions have changed. They do not assume that the problem with terrorists can be solved so easily, as supposedly was the case with the Soviet regime when it was stated that simply laying bare the follies of the Soviet ideology would make the Soviet people similar to people in the West. In the case of Islamic terrorism, decisive actions would also be necessary. And these actions were indeed implemented as the wars in Afghanistan and in Iraq show. However, these actions are not limited to external conflicts but also have direct implications for internal American life.

There has been a dramatic increase of the power of the federal government and the new Department of the Homeland Security. There are apparent limits on constitutional liberties, and some measures (e.g., creation of the military tribunal) could be easily compared with the actions of a totalitarian government. While it is true that this government control has evoked a stream of critical articles, what could be called the "silent majority" have not been very critical of these actions. One can assume that they do not mind the increase in governmental intrusiveness.

Of course, one must state that intellectuals have not directly reconsidered the role of totalitarian governments, for example the Soviet regime, as a force that can provide security and stability. Yet they are obviously moving in this direction. It is thought, for example, that an empire (American empire in this case) can sometimes be regarded as a positive phenomenon, even if it involves rule over a people against their wills. It is implied here that imperial presence is essential for stability. It is recognized that democracy does not always work, and that power might be imposed from above, as in the case of Iraq where democratic institutions could lead to the rise of a fundamentalist regime. All these intellectual trends provide the incentive for a reevaluation of the role of totalitarian regimes in non-modern and non-Western societies and cast doubt on the theory of all totalitarian regimes as the product of ideology. The new conditions also require reevaluation of the role of some previous regimes' relationships to society.

There is no doubt that ideology has played an important role in the historical process and that various ideological paradigms have occupied a central position in certain totalitarian regimes. Some of the actions of these regimes (e.g., the Holocaust) cannot be understood in the context of the geopolitical rationale. In fact, they were counterproductive to the regime's stated goals—maintaining power and expansion of empire. Yet ideology often obscured the real roles of the regimes, which in some modifications have played an important role in the stability of society. In many ways their desire to establish order caused their internal terror and intrusiveness in all aspects of human life.

To emphasize the importance of the fear of disorder but not the ideology in the formation of the totalitarian regime, I will focus attention on late medieval/early modern France in the fourteenth to sixteenth centuries. This case demonstrates how fear of disorder, of asocial processes, led to the emergence of a brutal absolutist state with features and policies strikingly similar to totalitarian regimes in the USSR and China.

This work deals with the totalitarian, or to be precise, the proto-totalitarian system as the product of the reality of fourteenth- through sixteenth-century Europe in general and France in particular. France, like many countries in Europe, was in a process of asocial/political transformation that in many cases was nothing but a societal meltdown aggravated by the Hundred Years War.

Asocial behavior spread to all segments of the society, in all forms, and led to the brutish response by the state. The range of punishment—its totality and cruelty—could well be compared with the actions of a totalitarian government. In its relentless drive to "normalize" society, the state actively regulated social life and even more intimate aspects of the people's lives, including their sexual lives. There were drives for regulation of the economy and even some aspects of social engineering, for example, attempts to populate the emerging colonial empires with exiles and produce "new men" and "new women" through a "reeducation" process that included hard physical labor and ideological indoctrination.

This increase in harshness in dealing with the populace, in fact, the emergence of a new sort of bondage, was combined with a twisted humanitarianism and a rudimentary safety net. Taken separately these elements can all be found in the democratic societies of the modern West, although in aggregate they should be regarded as features of totalitarian regimes of the modern era and of other types of regimes such as Oriental despotism.

The proto-totalitarian features in the early French monarchy cannot be attributed to the nefarious influence of ideology. France's kings were not aware of any socialist doctrine. Moreover, capitalism was in an embryonic state. Thus, the influence of capitalist ideology with its spirit of "control and punishment," as Foucault claims, should not be exaggerated. The role of the imperial drive for centralized power in the hands of the monarchy should not be exaggerated either. Indeed, France at that time was more preoccupied with sheer survival than with imperial aggrandizement. It was asocial processes in various forms that played the central role in late medieval and early modern France, and one can assume that this attempt to "normalize" society was a major reason for the early monarchy's engaging in activities similar to those of totalitarian governments.

While regarding the asocial drive as the important reason for the emergence of the semi-totalitarian, early modern, absolutist monarchies, the book also addresses the question of the effectiveness of these measures. The following conclusion can be reached. Although repressive/controlling state policy reduces the level of disorder, it is not a magic bullet. Several centuries are required for the results to be clearly visible. Moreover, these results are the work not only of the repressive system but also of the emerging civil society. Paradoxically enough, the semi-totalitarian early European monarchies created the conditions for the spreading of the security of people as well as their property and upheld the sacredness of the law in its universal application. All these were preconditions for the emerging civil society, and in the future this society would have no need of the absolutist state, and would itself acquire the Hobbesian essential, the ability to "control and punish," and thus ensure basic security for all of its members.

1

Asocial Processes in the Context of Early Modern European History

The early modern state had a difficult problem dealing with asocial/criminal behavior because such behavior was interwoven with many other political and social processes. Building a centralized monarchy marked a method of dealing with the problem. Centralization provided the state with a variety of mechanisms for dealing with problems. A standing army was the most important. Rudimentary police forces were also in the process of creation. These provided rulers with opportunities for foreign wars and means to check external aggression. They were also important for attempts to impose order internally. The meaning of order was in many cases hardly separable from the task of imposing it. Imposing order implicitly meant subduing social forces that opposed the centralized authority of the state. Expansion of the state's power was often done at the expense of the lower classes, but it would be overly simplistic to assume that the state acted exclusively as the representative of the elite or was driven by the interests of the bureaucratic machinery. The policy was manifold and controversial.

Centralization of the state and the rise of bureaucratic apparatus led to increased taxation and pressure over the populace. The populace, mostly the peasantry, also resisted the feudal lords. In the suppression of the peasantry, the state acted as an agent of the elite. At the same time the state engaged in the suppression of other manifestations of social resistance, not from the masses but actually from the elite. The state (France is a perfect example) engaged in subduing feudal barons who tried to play independent roles. In this capacity the state did not fight as an agent of the elite, but acted in many ways as an independent force. It of course, relied on the support of other groups—some segments of the middle class, gentry, etc.

The state pursued the same contradictory policy in dealing with the church. On the one hand the state was engaged in fighting against the church as a transnational institution. The goal was to sever or weaken the ties between the church and Rome and incorporate the church into the state structure. On the other hand, the state also engaged in strengthening official religion—religious beliefs approved by the state—because it helped keep the populace in check. The state also faced foreign challenges. Here it acted as both an aggressive and a defensive force.

Historians have widely studied these problems. But these were not the only ones faced by the state and embryonic civil society, which had started to develop with the rise of the cities. Several (to some extent mutually exclusive) processes accompanied the birth of modernity. One was the rise of the asocial process and the emergence and proliferation of groups that were against society in toto. The huge wave of asocial drives, destructive processes of various types, was possibly even stronger than the other challenges. The conflict between these groups and the state and society was one of the most important characteristics of the era.

Of course conflict between the state and asocial elements could not be always divorced from social conflicts. The institution attacked was not the abstract state, the institution to maintain order, but an institution with a well-defined social meaning. In fourteenth- through sixteenth-century France, maintaining control meant upholding a particular social order, the feudal society. Consequently, maintaining control and fighting crime maintained the power of the feudal elite. Another aspect of asocial behavior also made it difficult to see the asocial process as distinct from social conflicts. Quite a few criminals were members of the lower classes, and social conflicts, especially in the pre-modern/early modern era, often had criminal implications (looting, rape, etc.) These often blurred the lines between social conflicts and social outbursts.

The proliferation of these groups provided idiosyncratic features to what could be called the revolution of the fourteenth through sixteenth centuries. To understand the meaning of this revolution, one needs to apply a different definition from that usually used in modern western social sciences. The term revolution mostly means the transition from an old to a new order of social, political, and technological arrangements. This is how one usually analyzes such events as the "French Revolution," the "Industrial Revolution," the "Scientific Revolution." However, this notion—that revolution in France emerged comparatively recently, at the time of the French Revolution—is erroneous.

The term "revolution" before the eighteenth century usually means a rotation implying a change of the elite. It often also implies a change of dynasty and is related to social breakdown of the society, a push to general anarchy. The "revolutionary" aspects—transition to qualitatively new arrangements—were minimal. And only comparatively few people had social and political goals that could be defined in terms of social groups, classes, or parties in the modern sense.

Consequently, there was little of what could be called "class struggle" or political struggle as visualized in the modern West. It was true that these phenomena existed, and historians usually duly recorded them. Yet the important place these phenomena are usually allocated in historical research is often due not to their actual importance in the given period and country but to other considerations. It is usually due to the fact that the Western scientists, regardless of their professed creed and methodological affiliations, are bound to certain explanatory models of events that emphasize the role of well-defined sociopolitical groups or individuals, the carriers of power and particular ideologies. Consequently, the focus is usually on these aspects of phenomena even when they played comparatively minor roles in the process or competed with other factors. And this was the case with many premodern/non-Western revolutions, where asocial groups and drives were possibly even more important than well-defined social groups and political parties.

The role of these asocial groups and drives could be compared with "dark matter" in the cosmos, whose mass, though not visible, could be much larger than the mass of the visible planets and stars. Or, one could make a different analogy, to plankton in the sea. Plankton seem to be miniscule in comparison with whales and fish, yet the mass of plankton is immensely larger than the mass of all the other creatures in the ocean.

There were several indicators and characteristics of these asocial drives/groups. First, these groups saw little difference between the elite and the masses. In most cases they plundered, killed, and raped regardless of their victims' social position. That these criminals attacked the elite more often than the lower classes was not because they felt any deep-seated solidarity with the populace, but for more pragmatic reasons. One could get more from the rich than from the poor. Second, criminals were not just members of the lower classes. People of all ranks, even nobles, committed highway robbery. In fact, banditry was mostly an enterprise of the nobility. It was in tune with the tradition of the medieval elite, knight-warriors who lived by the sword.

Thus criminality, though in many ways enmeshed in social conflicts, for example, "social banditry," was often distinctly asocial. The asocial aspect of these processes made them the enemy not just of the elite but of society as a whole. One could define many processes in the early modern era as essentially asocial (directed not against particular social orders but against order itself) and see them as distinct phenomena. Crime was not the only manifestation of the asocial drive. It could be seen in sociobiological and purely biological aspects of human activities—sexual culture and personal hygiene. In all these cases asocial aspects were deeply interwoven in the daily life and had negative implications for the entire society. Consequently, the state, while fighting against these asocial processes, defended not just the interests of the elite but also those of society as a whole, including the lower classes. In this situation the position of the state was identical to the state's position in the protection of the people from a foreign threat.

Social Breakdown in the Era of the Hundred Years War

The rise of the strong absolutist state, with features sometimes similar to those of totalitarian regimes, could be seen in many parts of Europe. In many ways governments were responding to the social processes at the end of the late Middle Ages and early modern era. The pre-modern revolution had led not so much to changes in social and political arrangements as to a general meltdown. While this process spanned Europe, each society had its specific form. Danger often increased the drive for order, for example, when biosocial calamities such as pandemic diseases coincided with foreign invasions and the very existence of the country was at stake. This was the case with France in the late medieval/early modern era.

The transformation of a considerable part of the population in France into anomie, asocial bandits, was a result of a deep-seated process that might be traced to the High Middle Ages. France followed the European model; this process was highly accelerated by the fourteenth century for several reasons. First, the Hundred Years War led to the creation of armies of mercenaries. The nature of the war encouraged these mercenaries to lapse into banditry. It also led to a deep, prolonged dynastic crisis, and the vacuum at the top increased the sense of lawlessness that criminalized mercenaries and others used to their advantage. Second, the war coincided with the onslaught of the Black Death, with France one of the hardest hit countries in Europe. Periodic famines accompanied the Black Death, leading to further disintegration and facilitating banditry.

The profound crises into which France had lapsed cannot be understood outside its peculiar social and political context. Indeed, while the internal disintegration of the old *Gemeinschaft* social structure and foreign threats contributed to the proliferation of banditry, with the nobles playing an important role, it was not the only reason. The dynastic crisis and civil wars also contributed to the transformation of the nobles into highwaymen.

One needs to remember that there was often no actual "civil war" in the late medieval/early modern era. The term usually implies social conflict among well-defined social groups. In the late medieval/early modern era, "civil war" consisted of fighting between factions, usually united around various nobles or the king. These conflicts, structurally similar to gang warfare in modern times, were often not separate from pure banditry. All sides, whether led by nobles or not, engaged in looting, rape, and murder. Good examples of such events could be found if not in France, across the Channel in England. One observer notes: "Civil wars like those between the king and the barons in 1264-5 and 1321-2 may have resulted in elements of a defeated faction living a violent life outside the law for a time but the matter had not yet been properly examined."[1]

While thirteenth- and early fourteenth-century French nobles were spared from the shakeups that stimulated British nobles to follow the road of banditry, this changed in the second part of the fourteenth century, the time when France and England entered the Hundred Years War.

The immediate cause of the war was the death of Charles IV, the French king, in 1328. Edward III, the English king, regarded himself as the legitimate heir to the French throne, and this led to the long conflict. In the course of this conflict, France often had no legitimate authority, that is, a king recognized by the majority of the residents as the legitimate power. The power vacuum created the conditions of civil war in its premodern meaning: a power struggle among various factions for the throne or part of the realm. In France, it was the fight between Armagnacs and Burgundians. Complicated by the invasion of foreign troops and natural calamities like the Black Death, it led to deep social meltdown with proliferation of crime as one of its major manifestations.

Practically all groups of the population actively participated in violent crimes. But for the nobles banditry was a professional crime, so to speak. The pervasiveness of the nobles' criminality could be seen by the fact that even the king's direct involvement could not stop their activities. The power of the king, whether in France or England or other places in Europe, was often dependent on the personality of the ruler. Strong, charismatic kings could reduce the criminal vigor of the nobility. The king definitely enjoyed great prestige, and his presence could be a deterrent to criminal activity. Yet, a king, even a charismatic and powerful one, could not always stem the tide of crime committed by the nobles. The situation became even more serious in the case of the absence of formal restraint and when violent crime became a way of life. Indeed, the nobles a leading force in these criminal undertakings. They were leaders of detachments of mercenaries and other elements of the population, who were, while fighting for political goals, also engaged in wholesale looting. While the nobles were the organized force behind the various bands, the mercenaries were also among the major perpetuators of violent crimes. Indeed, over the course of the war, mercenaries often played a crucial role in the proliferation of banditry.

The mercenaries were the peculiar outcome of the social disintegration of the Late Middle Ages, when the familial relationships of the previous period were suffering constant erosion. Although nobles could be mercenaries, the definition was much broader and included quite a few people of common origins. By the end of the Middle Ages, personal serfdom was in the process of decline in France, and there were increasing numbers of young males of non-noble origins who had no alternative employment but to be mercenaries. The work was comparatively well paid and also quite prestigious, for warrior was the profession of the nobility-elite.

Thus, mercenaries, mostly young people, were in many ways responsible for the pervasive spread of violence in late medieval/early modern France. Indeed, while the culture of violence could be seen in all segments of society, it was not equally distributed among all members of the society. Age was a factor; younger people engaged in crime, including violent crime, much more often than did older people, and the vast majority of mercenaries were quite young.[2] Professional position was also important in predisposing people to violence. Indeed it was not so much social status as profession that made one group of people more violent than the other.[3] Yet, military people of all sorts were especially prone to act violently, and here the professional habits of mercenaries made them predisposed to banditry.[4]

Mercenaries as bandits were definitely not only a French problem. English mercenaries had acquired a taste for looting while engaged in the war in France. They returned to their homeland where they could apply their acquired skills and engage in various forms of criminal behavior.

While mercenaries and noble officers predominated in a variety of the banditry, it was not only they who were engaged in violent criminality.

This behavior was widespread among all groups of society, including clergy, students, and hordes of uprooted people such as vagabonds. Criminality as a behavior model had permeated all segments of society. In fact, the differences between the criminal and noncriminal worlds were in many cases blurred, and the behavior models of criminals such as bandits and the rest of the society were often essentially the same. This deep presence of criminal behavior among all groups of the population could be seen in various ways.

First, criminal violence was a sort of communal affair in which all groups of the population participated. This was, for example, the case with pogroms. One could see the direct connections between the rise of the banditry and the pogroms, for both events were in a way the product of social decomposition. All this indicated that the process of criminalization or banditry was caused by deep-seated social processes rather than some purely external event.

The pogroms also indicated a sort of cultural affinity between the various groups of the population. The pogrom as a form of looting and violence against the Jews was an enterprise in which all groups of the population, from nobles to vagabonds, could participate. It was not just that they had been united in their common belief that Jews were responsible for the suffering of Christ. The affinity was much deeper and indicated that looting and violence were seen as the appropriate way for everyone to act, from elite to common people.

Second, the deeply ingrained criminalization was manifested in the daily life of the people. All groups felt that freedom was equal to license and was implicitly connected with high position. This lack of inhibition was visible in a variety of ways, from throwing refuse into the street to sexual promiscuity and seeing rape as a legitimate form of sexual access.

The spread of asocial behavior of all types not only led to the spread of crime, often violent crime, but also had other biosocial implications. The asocial setting reinforced the biological problems. Pandemic diseases spread along trade routes. Merchants spread diseases by moving from one part of the globe to another; diseases were spread also by hordes of dirty vagabonds, mercenaries, and similar people who disregarded even the most rudimentary rules of hygiene. The filth that was an essential aspect of urban life facilitated the spread of disease. Even more than the Black Death, the spread of syphilis was essentially a social phenomenon, for it was directly connected with prostitution and promiscuity in general.

The deep asociality and the danger it entailed led to a peculiar, contradictory attitude on the part of the people to the idea of a strong power.

On one hand, power, actually any restraint, was hated. Power imposed taxes and asserted a social order in which the economic and political elite subdued the masses. Power restrained behavior, and all the people shared this dislike of restraint, from the elite to the lower classes. On the other hand, the same people deeply craved a strong power. The problem was that the absence of restraint not only provided opportunities for engagement in asocial behavior, but also created problems. The culture of criminality provided the opportunity not just to engage in banditry, but to be victimized by it. And the great calamities, such as the Hundred Years War, had taught the majority of the people that it was better to have brutal, strong rulers who would try to regulate one's life details than to have no ruler at all. And it was upon this feeling that the French monarchy built and expanded its power.

Orwellian Love: The King as "Big Brother"

There were various reasons for and interpretations of the emergence of the absolutist state in general and the French monarchy in particular. Fear of the asocial process, of crime first of all, played an important role in helping the rise of the absolutist state, but fear of anarchy also was a major reason that the idea of a strong monarchy was not challenged broadly for centuries. The idea that a strong king was essential for the survival of the nation was shared not only by the elite but also by the populace.

Most historians have seen major support for the king as stemming from the elite and bureaucracy. It seemed logical, for the king secured the existence of the feudal system from which the elite benefited. This vision of the French monarchy as representing and using its power to protect the ruling elite fits nicely into the Marxist assumption that the state is only the agent of the ruling elite. Its function is to protect their interests, using violence if necessary. In ancien régime France, this notion implied that the monarchy exercised its power mostly to protect the interests of the feudal lords and the upper echelon of the emerging third estate, the bourgeoisie. Upon the creation of modern society, the state started to represent the bourgeoisie. The Western liberal approach here was in many ways similar to the Marxist approach. The assumption was that, while in present Western democracies the state represents the majority of the people (government for the people and by the people), the situation was different in pre-revolutionary times; for example, the French kings represented the interests of the feudal and bureaucratic elite.

This theory could explain the dedication of the elite to the ruler, taking the term in its broad meaning, not only for protection of privileges but also because of the need of strong leaders for war. In some cases the role of the leader as warlord was seen as most essential because it promised victories and booty. The rise of the despotic Mongol khans shows that the elite voluntarily surrendered their rights to the khan.[5] Indeed, Mongols could not have engaged in their military exploits unless led by a leader with absolute power. At the same time, the paradigm implied that the despotic leader had a different relationship with the populace.

The monarchy was foreign to the populace, and this was one of the major reasons the people in their drive for freedom collided with the French ancien régime. Yet, along with the elite and the middle class, the general populace in early modern Europe usually had extremely favorable views of the monarch.

In some non-Western societies, this love for monarchs can be seen in the modern era as well. Richard Wortman states that Alexander III, one of the most reactionary tsars in Russian history, was quite popular among the Russian populace, and his death evoked a "truly national display of grief."[6] The populace could be quite critical about everything else in the social structure. They definitely hated the landlords and were often critical of the state bureaucracy, especially when it engaged in tax collecting. Yet there was no challenge of the authority of the king, because the idea of a society without a king as the supreme ruler was unthinkable. In France the people were ready to accept the idea that the king was divine or semi-divine, and this feeling rose among the populace during the late Middle Ages. By the beginning of the modern era, French kings started to acquire characteristics comparable to those of late Roman emperors and Hellenistic kings who projected the image of oriental rulers with no limitations in their power. It might not be accidental that French kings from these periods were fascinated by antiquity. The divine power of the Caesars and these kings was very likely a major reason for the attraction. And this divine power of the king, in many ways similar to that of totalitarian rulers, that ensured the "normalization" of society.

The King as Divine Person

Hobbes's theory of the absolutist ruler placed the ruler "entirely outside the system."[7] The king was a quasi-religious figure and there were increases in his sacred features from the Late Middle Ages onward.[8] Because of this divine role of the king, the crime of lèse-majesté was one of the most serious.[9] Judicial power emanated from the divine nature of royalty, and this was a major justification for regarding any outrage against magisterial power as a serious offense. It was severely punished from the fourteenth century onward.[10]

A vast majority of the French population subscribed to the divine, unlimited power of the king, along with having extremely high expectations from the king's personality. These attitudes, along with the adoration common folk felt for oriental rulers of the past and for totalitarian rulers of the twentieth century (for example, in Stalinist USSR), are perplexing to modern historians. French kings, like those rulers of the past and future, would abuse the populace through heavy taxation, hard work, and brutal punishment. That people should feel genuine love for a despot offends the essence of modern Western thinking, because it implies that average people approve of semi-slavery. In the minds of some, it could resonate similarly to the proposition that a wife should not mind being battered by her husband.

To avoid these problems, several arguments have been developed. The first could be placed in the context of the Marxist notion of "false consciousness." Social groups do not always understand their true interests and can be deceived by alien ideologies. The proletariat, for example, could be deceived by the ideology of the bourgeoisie and believe in the political and social values of the middle classes even when workers were actually exploited by the bourgeoisie. Marx regarded his major historical role as revealing the proletariat's real essence and developing an ideology for the workers. As soon as the workers acquired a true proletariat ideology, they would forsake the ideology of the middle class, with its concern for property rights and capitalist-type legality, and rise to achieve their political, social, and economic liberation.

The same theory is employed to understand people's love for despotic rulers of the distant or not so distant past. The assumption is that the masses were plainly unaware of the existence of political liberties, human rights in their modern Western reading. The repressive policy and deliberate attempts of the regimes to keep people ignorant can also be blamed. While the people believed in the necessity of a despotic rule due to their ignorance, the elite (this was the case with the elite in communist society) expressed love for the despots for other reasons. The elite were afraid of the ruler's wrath, and from here stems their Orwellian love for power. However, the idea of liberty was a "self-evident truth" that could not be kept from the human mind too long. Freedom is always preferable to slavery, and sooner or later, the people would find this truth and rise against the tyrants, as in the French Revolution and anti-communist revolution in 1991 Russia.

Another theory for the people's adoration for despotic rulers is often employed to explain the love of the common folk for modern despotic rulers, to explain the external adoration of the Soviet people for Stalin, for example. The proponents of this theory discard the notion that popular demonstrations of love for the ruler were the result of fear or ignorance, or that the people's enthusiasm was just a manifestation of double thinking (they express their external love for their leader but inwardly hate him at the same time). In the view of these historians, the Soviet people's love for Stalin was genuine. However, these historians, mostly from Western academia, believed that people cannot genuinely love a tyrant. So this genuine love for Stalin implied that he was not a despot. Following this line of thought these historians took at face value Soviet propaganda that a majority elected Stalin and other Soviet leaders who followed him, either directly or through the Communist Party. These historians were also prone to minimize the scope of Stalinist terror.

Yet these theories fail to provide an adequate explanation for the persistent adoration of the king as an institution in the minds of the populace, the people who seem to suffer most from absolutist rule. It is true that most French people in the sixteenth and seventeenth centuries were ignorant. Yet their educational level was not radically different from that of American settlers in the late eighteenth century. The American settlers could elaborate on their objections to the monarchy, and the American Revolution never seriously entertained the idea of monarchy as essential to the newborn state. A "self-evident truth" for one category of people in a certain period of time might not be a "self-evident truth" for others even at the same time. As to the second theory, one could entertain ideas about Stalin as a democratically elected leader on the basis of "elections," but this could not be said about French kings. They never claimed they were elected by the masses. Their legitimacy came from above: they were "god-anointed."

The almost universal assumption that the king's power should be absolute and receive legitimacy from above (god) can be explained only if one takes into account that most groups in society were extremely fearful of insecurity in its many manifestations, including crime. This fear of disorder, this vulnerability to the threat of chaos, was a major reason why the lower classes accepted the power of feudal lords. It is one of the most powerful reasons why a majority of the populace accepted and supported the idea of a strong, and if need be brutal state.

There was an instinctive view of the master as the protector. The instinct of obedience, according to some sociologists such as George Simmel, is an essential human attribute, regardless of time and place. "The majority of men not only cannot exist without leadership; they also feel that they cannot: they seek the higher power which relieves them from responsibility; they seek a restrictive, regulatory rigor which protects them not only against the outside world but also against themselves."[11] One could of course question Simmel's claim that this drive to submit to a strong ruler can be attributed to all people regardless of time and place. (One must also remember that Simmel himself admitted that this drive coexisted with other drives.) Still, this view of strong authority as prerequisite to the survival of society was part of popular psychology in the early modern era in Europe in general and in France in particular. Strong power was not only hated (the uprisings indicate this) but also loved. This popular love for the king explained the durability of the monarchy as an institution.

The monarchy could not have survived on coercion alone, and the relationship between the feudal lord and the peasantry was not based exclusively on coercion. It was based on a *Gemeinschaft* social contract, in which the ruler had an important responsibility. This was maintaining order, a guarantee for basic security. A threat to basic security could come not only from a foreign invasion but from an internal threat to security, to basic order. All classes from the lowest to the highest desired this order, and the king in many ways guaranteed its existence.[12]

All members of society, including the lower classes, needed freedom from predatory banditry. All members of society needed a dependable, safe water supply and control over the disposal of garbage and human refuse. Before civil society emerged with strong, self-controlled mechanisms, the authority of rulers was needed to ensure that basic rules of sanitation—without which the spread of pandemic diseases would be certain—would be upheld.

Because the presence of the king as a strong, cementing force was required, political play as it exists in the modern West was impossible. Removal of the king from the central role in the political structure would cause the disintegration of society and general chaos. If the king was removed, there followed at most an intermission before a new king was put in place. The strong ruler as the centerpiece of the political structure explained the wide spread of monarchy as an accepted form of government. The necessity of monarchy as an institution was hardly questioned by anyone. The remedy for problems was not to replace the monarchy with another institution, but rather to be sure the monarch was a good one. The qualities of a good monarch were a central theme of political thought, and although the positive characteristics might vary from culture to culture, every definition implied that a good monarch maintained order.

This explanatory model could be applied to early modern France and Europe in general, and provide a clue for the rise of the absolutist state, some of whose attributes and actions made it quite similar to the modern totalitarian state.

Maintaining Order as the King's Major Responsibility

The assumption that the king's major role was to defend his subjects had been an essential element of contracts between rulers and the ruled since the dawn of history. It was at the core of the ruler's legitimacy in the broad meaning of the word. It could be compared in importance only to the king's ability to protect his subjects from foreign threats. Combating crime was not merely a police matter, as John Bellamy has observed in his book *Crime and Public Order*: "At [its] heart were the crucial issues of the royal authority and the structure of the state, whether they were to survive in their existing forms or to wither away."[13]

This was an essential part of the French kings' vision of their social role since the time of the Middle Ages. For example, Louis VI, who in 1120 took the title *rex Franciae*--king of France--regarded "public defense" as his major responsibility.[14] This implied both defense against external enemies and maintaining public order. Yet, only toward the end of the Middle Ages and the beginning of the modern era, which marked the rapid proliferation of asocial behavior, did the term "public defense" acquire meaning. And this role in the pacification of the country helped increase the power of the French king. As Gauvard has stated, fear of crime "played a major role in the emergence of the French state at the end of the Middle Ages. Pursuit and punishment of criminals became a mandate for the French monarchy and, in turn, strengthened the control of the monarchy over the countryside."[15]

Henry Heller supports these assumptions and states that the rise of power and prestige of the French king was due not only to "dynastic ambition," but also to the development of means "to defend the kingdom from the English and also against the brigands who repeatedly infested the country."[16] The king's concern with basic order and his drive to impose this order was one essential reason kings were able to "impose themselves on their respective populations to an unprecedented degree."[17]

Of course, it goes without saying that the king's maintaining a certain social and political order benefited the elite. Yet there was no partiality in the sense that social and political status of the victims affected the status of the crime.[18] Thus, it is overly simplistic to see the drive for order as a force that benefited only the elite or the monarchy as an institution. It had a much broader appeal. Order benefited all segments of the population, including the lower classes. And it was hardly accidental that the king visualized himself as "protector of 'common people.'"[19] The king was "publicly responsible for preserving the *tranquillitas regni*. Ever since the early Middle Ages, the *raison d'être* of monarchical authority had been the king's function as preserver of the peace and dispenser of justice. Any infraction of the peace such as a private war was therefore an injury to the king, albeit an indirect one, and could be [likened] to treason."[20] In pre-modern France the monarchy did not exist separately from the body of the king, and therefore the king's personality was the essential foundation of the political and social order.[21] His personal presence was needed to ensure the unity and order of the realm.[22] Kings did not avoid their responsibilities as major anchors of public order, and they understood the importance of their presence in court. Bellamy states: "The beneficial effect of the royal presence at the scene of the crime, at the trial, or at any rate in the region where the disturbances had centered was an acknowledged fact."[23] A king was very much aware of this, and traveled great distances, especially when "he was particularly keen to have a verdict of 'guilty' returned against the accused."[24]

The king's presence in the country was essential for maintaining order. His prolonged absence from the realm had a negative implication for the entire judicial system in any European society of that time. For example, the absence of the English king (mostly because of the war with France) from the realm had a negative impact on maintaining order. The war and other absences adversely affected public order and led to asocial fragmentation on both political and social levels. Bellamy says, "when the English monarch left his kingdom for any length of time in order to seek out his foreign adversaries, lawlessness and disorder were very likely to increase."[25]

The king's personality was important not just for maintaining the law; he was to some degree the embodiment of the law. According to Claude Gauvard, who has written on the fear of crime in France during the Middle Ages, it was assumed that the "king should serve as an example."[26] Spiritual wholesomeness was needed not just for the king, but also for the capital, Paris, as the place of the king's residence.[27]

Thus, the lower and middle classes and a majority of the elite accepted the idea of a strong and, if needed, brutal state. All sections of the population feared the consequences of anarchy, with criminality as one of its most salient manifestations. This was a consensus that all social groups shared despite their mutual animosity. Even the most brutish social conflicts European states experienced in the early modern era did not change the attitude of the majority of the population, of all classes, in regard to the idea of a strong state. One might even suggest that the experience of great calamities, such as the Hundred Years War, reinforced in the minds of the majority the necessity for a brutal state to normalize society and provide private and basic security for its members. Indeed, the notion that the state provided protection for individual subjects regardless of social position was implicit in the social contract. (The only exception could be slaves who were outside societal protection, but the institution of slavery or even bondage disappeared almost completely in most countries of the West.)

This peculiar element of the social contract existed despite the animosity between various groups of the population. These conflicts between social groups did not prevent them from cooperation, for as Simmel has correctly stated, these conflicts are also a form of social development.[28] This aspect of the relationship between rulers and subjects as a holistic unity implied that the ruler should provide conditions of a safe environment for the subjects when the subjects abrogated all rights to be engaged in state affairs. This essential aspect of normality included, first of all, protection of the human body from direct violence such as death, mutilation, or rape. This basic security was of concern for all segments of society, from the lowest pauper to the king himself. Later, these basic guarantees of normality would include protection of property rights and contractual obligations in general.

Related to the problem of internal security was the problem of foreign threats. And the ruler was expected to protect the state from foreign threats. Foreign threats could be seen as another manifestation of the asocial process, since roaming hordes of mercenary bandits plagued the countryside. In the process of dealing with these asocial processes, the king acquired strong, totalitarian types of power in both civic societies and absolutist states. All these structures used this power in various ways in fighting asocial processes.

Residents of the late medieval/early modern state also experienced a bio-threat—pandemic diseases that were also often related to asocial behavior. So, in the process of widening the area of security and order, the authorities imposed quarantines and implemented elements of sanitation. All these actions provided the conditions needed for survival of all members of society. This is the basis of the social contract, in both pre-modern and modern times. The difference, of course, was that in pre-modern states power guaranteed the security of the people. The brutal state was in most cases the only solution, the reason why, despite its many abuses, societies throughout Europe required the existence of a strong government and, implicitly, feudal order.

The Problem of Normalization: Repressive Models and Asocial Groups

The problem of asocial behavior and the crucial importance of strong government could be seen in non-Western societies as well. But in the West the state was especially tough in dealing with crime. Criminals were repressed or exterminated. The rise of the legalistic culture in Western societies constrained the state's ability to deal with crime in the way many non-Western societies did. The Western state did not have the flexibility to "incorporate" criminals into the state structure, because in legalistic societies the notion developed that the law is above everyone, including the ruler. This notion was directly related to the development of private property.

The Law as Quasi-Religion

The notion of legality was slowly incorporated into the political and social culture of the European state and changed the approach to the law and those who broke the law. These changes were slow and influenced first of all the royal power itself. They slowly made the king the high priest of a new quasi-religion—the law.

The notion that the ruler must maintain order and not be engaged in criminal behavior was common knowledge within the ruling class. Machiavelli stated that the power of authority would be undermined if one did not "refrain from laying hands on the property of his citizens and subjects, and on their womenfolk."[29] As time progressed, this pragmatic notion of statecraft was slowly transformed into the high call of power, and law started to acquire the features of religion. One of the most profound changes in the perception of royalty at the dawn of the modern era was the notion that law transcended the ruler's personality and could not be reduced to the king's whims.

Nor were the execution of justice and the role of the judges separate from the idea of the law as sacred. The function of the law was seen in this way from the beginning of world history. The sacredness of the law was not seen here in the narrow sense that the practitioner of the law should strictly follow the letter of the codes. Judgment was made valid, not through the formal framework of justice but through a sense of duty, a desire to be just in a deep religious sense, with total separation of judgment from the personal interests of the judge. In the feudal era, litigious parties could appeal to the feudal lord for a verdict not only because they thought the lord had better knowledge, but also because they trusted his moral caliber. They approached him the same way as they would a priest. And the judgment of the lord was expected not to be arbitrary.[30]

The assumption that law is not entirely the whim of the ruler was present in pre-modern and non-Western thought. A prophet reproached King David of the Old Testament for taking the wife of another man. Agamemnon was condemned for taking Achilles' concubine. Yet in pre-modern and non-Western societies, despite all the assertions about the sacredness of the law, the law was often dissolved to the will of the king. In oriental despotism the will of the king actually became the law. Only in modern Europe did the law emerge as a truly divine force, almost equal to religion in nature. The law ruled society and even the king, whose major role was to maintain the law. The notion of the sacredness of the law and the related notion of the universality of the applicability of the law ruled ancien régime France.

Of course, it is true that the nature of the ancien régime's social/political structure de-universalized the law and weakened its application in many cases, because it was still a pre-modern society and different segments of society had different rights. "Roughly speaking, one might say that, under the ancien Régime each of the different social strata had its margin or tolerated illegality: the non-application of the rule, the non-observance of the innumerable edicts ordinances was a condition of the political and economic functioning of society."[31]

The application of the law thus depended on a variety of factors. Occasionally, it was just the whim of the authorities, who for various reasons decided not to prosecute those who ignored the law. For example, owing to the nature of the feudal system, for some privileged estates and various corporate bodies the legal difference from other cases was an integral part of the social contract. In this case, disregard of certain aspects of the law was legitimized in its own way. It sometimes took on statutory form—as with the privileges accorded certain individuals and groups—that made certain conduct for certain groups not so much as illegal as exempt. "Sometimes it took the form of massive general non-observance, which meant that for decades, sometimes for centuries, ordinances could be published and constantly renewed without ever being implemented. Sometimes it was a matter of laws gradually falling into abeyance."[32]

However, even taking all these considerations into account, one could state that by the beginning of the modern era (fifteenth through sixteenth century) the law had increased its rigidity in dealing with crimes that undermined the existence of society. These included attacks on life and property as well as direct or indirect attacks on the foundation of the state. By the beginning of the centralized French monarchy, we see the divinization of the law, translated into the concept that the sacred duty of the state was to protect the life and property of its subjects. This sense of the sacredness of the law as a guarantor of the population's daily existence justified the ruler's power. And while elements of this could be found in the *raison d'être* of oriental rulers, for example the Ottoman sultans, it was elaborated in the West, especially in France, due to the growth of the legalistic culture rooted in the emerging notion of private property.

The legalistic rigor of the early modern state and its vision of justice and the law as divine and immutable made it different not just from earlier eras of European history, but also, to some degree, from totalitarian states in the twentieth century. Twentieth-century political scientists could be quite flexible in regard to the application of the law. Carl Schmitt, for example, has stated that this flexibility often depended on the interests of the ruler, and emphasized the notion that law be "devoid of any sacred content."[33] This approach was definitely foreign to the judicial thought of early modern Europe, including France.

Leo Strauss has stated that Schmitt misread Hobbes as the proponent of totalitarian regimes that had no limitation and could violate any law. According to Strauss, the view of Hobbes and other political thinkers of that era was that justice was sacred and the absolute power of the state was needed to uphold it. "Whereas in the final instance Hobbes brings out the natural and therefore innocent evil, so that evil may be combated, Schmitt speaks with unmistakable sympathy of an 'evil' which is no longer to be taken in the moral sense. This sympathy is nothing other than admiration for animal power."[34] Schmitt's relativistic immorality and Hobbes's stringent emphasis on the sacredness of the law were due to the social settings in which they developed their theories.

Strauss detailed the differences, stating that Schmitt regarded the world as a conflict between social groups and the state, and Hobbes saw the same world as the endless conflict among particular individuals.[35]

Schmitt lived in the modern West, with a strong civic society and strong socialization of individuals in particular groups, which prevented the majority from lapsing into asocial behavior. This stability of the basic social interaction provided Schmitt and the Nazi state (whose ideologies he was to be engaged in) with the attitude of relativistic amorality in high politics. In the case of Hobbes, the situation was altogether different. The level of socialization was weak. Society was not so much a place of conflicting groups as an asocial "anomie" of individuals. The basic rules of social interaction were flouted, so the state approached the law as the basis for interaction in human society with exemplary rigor. In this context, the law as morality should be viewed as quasi-religion and judges as quasi-priests. There was no dichotomy between raison d'état and moral imperative, for moral imperative in religious strictness was raison d'état.

By the sixteenth century there was an increasing feeling that "justice was divine in its importance."[36] The divinization of the process of justice had led to visions of the judge as a semi-priestly figure. As Coopland stated, judges were people of strong moral authority. "They inflicted punishments from which the mind turns away in self-defense."[37] Yet they did so because they considered it their duty to maintain order in society, and they regarded inflicting these terrible punishments as fulfilling their duties. "Many of them were what could be called, in the obsolete phases, 'God-fearing men.'"[38] By the sixteenth century the judicial machinery mostly received their jobs "according to their merits and knowledge."[39] Morality was of the utmost import. In the sixteenth century, it was stated that for a judge, "knowledge and eloquence are less needed than good morals, gravity, majesty, and decency" and "The basis of their authority was almost entirely moral."[40] This vision of the law as enmeshed in religion began to place the law above the king.

A sense of legality restricted early modern European rulers. The law, at least in its major aspects such as protection of life and property, was above everyone, including the king, who became a sort of high priest of the state and the law. The process that transformed the French king into the high priest of the law took several centuries, and finally led to what is characterized as "two bodies of the king." The king was considered to have two embodiments. As a mortal, he was subject to the vagaries of the flesh and died as all mortals do. Like all mortals, he was subject to divine judgment a final accountability for his deeds. The other aspect of the king was his legalistic divinity. The king as final guarantor of the law and order never died.

This emphasis on the immortality of the king as the manifestation of the law became quite pronounced from the end of François I's reign on. Even his funeral arrangement emphasized his immortality as the embodiment of the law. "After the death of François I the perpetuity of his supreme office was expressed by an effigy of the dead king, like a life-size doll, dressed in red like the lawyers of the Paris Parlement. This remarkably life-like imitation, held high as if walking upright, had an important place in the procession of the dead king. The scarlet-robed members of the Parlement accompanied the majestic doll; both the figure of the king and those who accompanied it thus followed the practices adopted at the end of previous reigns. The absence of mourning and black garments was underlined by the brilliant clothing of the magistrates, expressing better than any speech the immortality of justice, the prime constituent of the crown and of the external and imperishable body of the king."[41] And the protection of the law immortalized the king's body and provided the view of the king as "a semi-priestly figure."[42] The function of protector of the law and therefore of the foundation of the social and political order could compete only with the role of the king as warlord.[43]

In his immortal capacity, the king provided a guarantee of the law of the state. These eternal aspects of the royal personality justified the royal power. Contained within this notion was the implication that the king could not break the law. To do so would contradict his eternal essence. If he did so, the king would delegitimize himself, transforming himself into a "tyrant" who could be deposed despite the legitimacy of his inherited succession to the throne and his coronation. The notion of "tyrant" versus legitimate king entered political discourse in the early modern era.

There was already in the fifteenth and sixteenth centuries a clear notion that the king must be different from tyrants, that is, from people who only followed their own desires. A tyrannical ruler could not rule the country well and would bring nothing but misfortune to his subjects.[44] The king could enjoy absolute power only to the extent that he played the role of defender of the law. The law in its major faculties—the "natural law"—was immutable.

The rising expectations of the king as guarantor of the law coexisted with the rising notion of the absolute power of the king. In some cases, of course, the latter notion contradicted the legalistic nature of eternal royal power. Increasingly, however, the notion of the absolute power of the king reinforced the notion of the legalistic culture as the reason for the king's existence. The king needed absolute power for a very simple reason: without it he would have been unable to maintain the law. The king also needed absolute power to strictly divide the legal from the illegal. Paradoxically enough, the rise of the king's power in the context of legalistic discourse at the same time limited his power. In particular, the emerging legalistic nature of the state made it impossible to incorporate members of the criminal world into the elite. The differences between criminal and "straight" had already been made clear, so the chief of a large band of highway robbers could not be a part of the state council, even if he was a noble. The notion of legality limited the ways modern rulers could approach criminals. The ruler could not incorporate them into the elite even in cases of political expediency for the same reason he could not break the basic laws of the realm.

However, while fulfilling his major societal obligation, the protection of order from both internal and external threats, the king could enjoy absolute power. At least this was a view among some political thinkers in sixteenth-century France. Jean Bodin (1530-1596), one of the principal ideologists of the absolutist state, made this clear in his "Six Books of the Commonwealth, 1576." He stated, "'the absolute power of the sovereign prince and seigneurs does not in any way extend to the laws of God and of nature.' In short, divine and natural law bound the sovereign prince as much as they bound the subject. The king, through the mechanism of the central state, had the obligation to make sure his subjects obeyed divine and natural laws (as well as his laws); alas for them, while the king was bound by these laws, no human agency could hold him to them."[45]

The king thus not only had the right to be all-powerful, he could not opt for another role. "Tyrannical" rulers—those who exhibited cruelty for their own whims—demonstrated one type of deviation from the right path; weak kings who shunned the exercise of power represented the other form. As the only foundation of the social and political order, the king was to be strong. Some jurists of that time "attacked a weak monarchy that would not or could not affect a reform of the judicial system."[46] They pushed the king toward increasingly brutal punishments.

The Problem of Incorporation:
Oriental State Versus Western State

In the modern West in general and in early modern France in particular, the rigor of the law and the strict division of criminal from noncriminal behavior required the most resolute dealing with criminals. The story was different in pre-modern/non-Western states. There, the sense of the law, as a universal principle, was weak and often reduced to the will of the ruler, and the incorporation of the criminal into the elite could be seen as an option.

By the beginning of the modern era in Western Europe, the law emerged as a force that conditioned the behavior of the king. The law in quasi-religious form provided the final justification for the ruler's absolute power. The absolute power of the law, not his volition, provided the final justification for his rule. It was a different story with pre-modern and oriental states, where the rulers were equated with the law, in fact, were the law.[47] Karen Barkey pointed out that this made it possible for these rulers to incorporate some of the most prominent bandits into the elite and by doing this, ease the pressure on the state. This could be seen in the Ottoman state.[48]

Barkey provided information that clearly demonstrates that the Ottoman state was quite aware of the danger of anarchy and would resort to force in dealing with the problems that erupted in the sixteenth through seventeenth centuries; in this the Ottomans did precisely the same as the French rulers. "Whether religious student or mercenary, the state initially treated all rural disruptions in the same manner. It consistently sought to increase control of the center over the rural areas, bypassing regional state officials feared to have developed an alternative basis of power. To accomplish this goal, the state expanded its military forces" (156). In some cases the government was able to muster enough force to use the utmost brutality in dealing with the rebels. In Anatolia, the state seemed to have enough resources at the beginning of the seventeenth century, and "Peace returned to the provinces only after a confrontation between the state and bandits during which Grand Vizier Kuyucu Murad Pasha deployed strong and well-trained armies to slaughter the *celalis* (1606-7). In one clash, it is said that 20,000 heads were heaped in front of the grand vizier's tent" (153). Yet the state was not always able to gain the upper hand. "The banditry subsided for a while, to emerge again in 1622 under new leadership (Abaza Mehmet Pasha and later Abaza Hasan Pasha) but a similar constituency. These events were suppressed in 1658 when a new dynasty of grand viziers reestablished strong state control of the provinces" (153).

The Ottomans experienced problems with rebels and, in this case, opted to incorporate bandits into the state structure. In many cases the explanation of the problems was simple enough—lack of force was a major problem. In other cases the Ottomans seemed to be locked into a no-win situation. On the one hand, the rulers increased the numbers of troops that could be used in foreign adventures as well internal threats and, while the government pushed for stability, it ironically added "to the number of potentially rebellious armed mercenaries" (156). On the other hand, the sultan might co-opt the leader of the outlaws and by doing so check any further proliferation of asocial violence that could threaten the regime's existence.

While the lack of force was one of the major reasons for this policy, it was not the only one. The cultural aspect of this incorporation should not be ignored (e.g., the absence of a strict definition of legal and illegal as developed in Western Europe), and it would be wrong to assume that there was nothing special in the Ottoman political culture, oriental in its essence, which implied that the state would engage in negotiations and incorporations, even when it could have employed sufficient force. Force was the most acceptable way of dealing with rebels, but not the only acceptable way. In the Ottoman Empire, unlike medieval Europe, legal discourse was weak and the difference between legal and illegal was not sharply perceived. Incorporating criminals into its ranks, Barkey claimed, was essentially the way the state grew and. "The power of the state necessarily grew not only at the expense of social groups but also because the state incorporated or legitimized these groups and linked them to itself" (1). In these situations, the state could proceed with its combination of coercion and incorporation. Barkey claimed that Ottoman sultans saw disturbances "as opportunities for bargaining, initially reaching into the state's revenues, distributing patronage to buy off or channel new emerging opposition. Only later did sultans resort to force. Even the pervasive banditry was less often crushed by force than it was managed by widespread bargaining" (2).

Barkey claimed that the Ottoman way of dealing with antisocial elements through incorporation was a result of the Ottoman state having a less coercive political culture than that of Western states. She also stated that these coercive elements in the political and social order were not often needed, for the banditry was of no real threat to the state. Elaborating on various antisocial groups, she stated that "neither the religious groups nor the mercenaries actually became a threat to the state" (156).

Barkey concluded by reiterating this point and stating that the ability to absorb criminal elements was a sign of flexibility in the Ottoman state, and that here the Ottoman state demonstrated superiority to the European state. She found out (quite rightly) that the ability to integrate asocial elements into the state was due to Ottoman political culture, which did not differentiate clearly between legal right and legal wrong. "The western distinctions between legitimacy and illegitimacy became blurred" (239). Actual criminalization of the political and social culture, where legitimacy had been defined through force and force alone, is regarded as a sign of strength.

Barkey stated that the French did not follow the model of the Ottomans, and strictly defined what was acceptable and not acceptable. Europeans paid dearly for the legalistic rigor that accompanied the French rigorous pursuit of centralization: "In France, the state first worked to exclude from the realm of the state all regional power holders, and only much later did it develop the policy and ideology of inclusion" (241). The state paid for this rigorous legalism, for "the French state had been toppled and replaced through a bloody revolution." This could have been avoided if European states in general, and the French state in particular, had exhibited the sort of legalistic relativism that could be seen in the Ottoman state, actually all non-European nations. "The western states therefore could have benefited from Ottoman's example, but they (and many analysts) did not see it for what it was, as strength rather than weakness."

Barkey in a curious way proceeded to accuse French rulers, European rulers in general, of "political incorrectness" (an inability to abandon a Western-oriented point of view). This pervasive "political incorrectness" was the crux of the problem. She stated that if the French rulers had understood in the depths of their hearts the wisdom of the Oriental model, the fate of the French monarchy could have been different, yet the "Ottoman route would likely have seemed below the rigid dignity of European monarchs" (241). However, one should not view Ottoman rulers as absolutely different from Western rulers. Ottoman and other Oriental rulers had the same concern as Western ones—to eliminate crime and ensure the basic security of their subjects. And those who were not able to secure stability were hardly popular among their subjects.[49] It is clear, then, that in their approach to the banditry Ottoman rulers were not much different from Western rulers. Still, they might be more lenient to criminals in comparison to Western rulers because of the streak of legal nihilism in Ottoman culture. One should question whether this legalistic nihilism, the tolerance of the Oriental state, was a sign of strength.

These asocial movements, with banditry as a prime manifestation, were mortal enemies of society and of the state. These processes prevented economic progress and were major reasons why the Ottoman state lagged behind European powers and finally lost in a confrontation with them. Modern Turkey reemerged as a strong state only when Turkey abandoned the system of legalistic flexibility and turned to Western rigor in dealing with crime.

Notes

1. John Bellamy, *Crime and Public Order in England in the Latter Middle* Ages (London: Routledge, 1973), 10.
2. Benoit Garnot, "La perception des délinquants en France du XIVe au XIXe siècle," *Revue Historique* (1996): 352-53.
3. Nicole Gonthier, *Délinquance, justice et société dans le Lyonnais médiéval: de la fin du XIIIe siècle* (Paris: Editions Arguments, 1993), 157.
4. Claude Gauvard, *"De grace especial": crime, état et société en France à la fin du Moyen Age* (Paris: Publications de la Sorbonne, 1991), 532.
5. George Vernadsky, *The Mongols and Russia/Mongoly i Rus'* (Tver': Lean/Agraf, 1997), 127.
6. Richard S. Wortman, *Scenarios of Power: Myth and Ceremony in Russian Monarchy*, 2 vols. (Princeton: Princeton University Press, 1995-2000), 2: 298.
7. Talcott Parsons, *The Structure of Social Action: A Study in Social Theory with Special Reference to a Group of Recent European Writers* (New York: Free Press, 1964), 314.
8. Pascale Thibault, "Louis XII, de l'impérator au père: du peuple: inconographie du regne et de sa mémoire," *Nouvelle Revue du XVIe Siècle* 13, 1 (1995): 31; Emmanuel Le Roy Ladurie, *The Royal French State: 1460-1610* (Oxford: Blackwell, 1987), 1.
9. Le Roy Ladurie, *The Royal French State*, 946.
10. Maurice Bauchond, *La justice criminelle du magistrat de Valenciennes au moyen âge* (Paris: Picard, 1904), 212.
11. George Simmel, *On Individuality and Social Forms* (Chicago: University of Chicago Press, 1971), 103.
12. The idea that the middle class needed the strong authority of the king was much in vogue in Marxist historiography. Soviet historians emphasized that the middle classes were concerned with the free flow of services and goods. Only strong royal power provided enough stability to facilitate this, and this was the major reason for middle-class support of the monarchy.
13. Bellamy, *Crime and Public Order*, 1.
14. James B. Collins, "State Building in Early Modern Europe: The Case of France," *Modern Asia Studies* 31, 3 (1997): 606.
15. Claude Gauvard, "Fear of Crime in Late Medieval France," in *Medieval Crime and Social Control*, ed. Barbara A. Hanawalt and David Wallace (Minneapolis: University of Minnesota Press, 1999), 1.
16. Henry Heller, "The French Nobility and the State in the Late Middle Ages," *Canadian Journal of History* 12, 1 (1977): 2. On the importance of royal power in the drive against crime in the sixteenth century, see also Robert Muchembled, "Anthropologie de la violence dans la France moderne (XVe-XVIIIe siècle)," *Revue de Synthèse* 108, 1 (1987): 47, 51.
17. K. A. Stanbridge, "England, France and Their North American Colonies: An Analysis of Absolute State Power in Europe and in the New World," *Journal of Historical Sociology* 10 (March 1997): 28.
18. Nicole Gonthier, *Le châtiment du crime au Moyen Age* (Rennes: Presses Universitaires de Rennes, 1998), 29.
19. Benoit Garnot, "La legislation et la repression des crimes dans la France moderne (XVIe-XVIIIe siècle)," *Revue Historique* 293, 1 (1995): 88.
20. S. H. Cuttler, *The Law of Treason and Treason Trials in Later Medieval France* (Cambridge: Cambridge University Press, 1981), 19; on the role of the king as the force which maintains order and renders justice, see also Gonthier, *Le châtiment du crime*, 84.

21.   Roland Mousnier, "Les fidelités et les clientèles en France aux XVIe, XVIIe et XVIIe siècles," *Histoire Sociale/Social History* 15 (Mai/May 1982): 37; Malcolm C. Smith, "Opium of the People: Numa Pompilius in the French Renaissance," *Bibliothèque d'Humanisme et Renaissance* 3, no. 52, 1 (1990): 9; F. G. Pariset, "Réflexions sur les origines du classicisme français," *Bulletin de la Société d'Histoire Moderne* 59, 15-16 (1961): 18; Ellery Schalk, "Under the Law or Laws unto Themselves: Noble Attitudes and Absolutism in Sixteenth- and Seventeenth-Century France," *Historical Reflections/Relexions Historiques* 15, 1 (1988): 282.

22.   Jean Boutier, Alain Dewerpe, and Daniel Nordman, "Les voyages des rois de France," *L'Histoire* 24 (1980). See also R. J. Knecht, *French Renaissance Monarchy: Francis I and Henry II* (London: Longman, 1996), 74. The importance of the king for the order and unity of the realm was a major reason for the French king in the sixteenth century to move from one place to another. Sometimes his personal presence was needed for the work of the judicial machinery.

23.   Bellamy, *Crime and Public Order*, 11.

24.   Ibid., 12. While the quoted cases were about England, the same could be said about France.

25.   Ibid., 10.

26.   Gauvard, "Fear of Crime," 24; Gauvard, *"De grace especial"*, 224-25.

27.   *"De grace especial"*, 274.

28.   Simmel, *On Individuality*, 23, 70.

29.   Machiavelli, *The Prince* (Cambridge: Cambridge University Press, 1988), 59.

30.   Jean Delumeau and Yves Lequin, *Les malheurs des temps: histoire des fléaux et des calamités en France* (Paris: Larousse, 1987), 123.

31.   Michel Foucault, *Discipline and Punish: The Birth of the Prison* (New York: Pantheon, 1977), 82.

32.   Ibid.

33.   Carl Schmitt, *State, Movement, People: The Tragic Structure of the Political Unity: The Question of Legality* (Corvallis: Plutarch Press, 2001), 16-17, 63.

34.   Leo Strauss, "Comments on Carl Schmitt's *Der Begriff des Politischen*," in *Carl Schmitt: The Concept of the Political* (New Brunswick: Rutgers University Press, 1976), 97.

35.   Ibid., 88.

36.   Jonathan L. Pearl, *The Crime of Crimes: Demonology and Politics in France, 1560-1620* (Waterloo: Wilfrid Laurier University Press, 1999), 130-31.

37.   G. W. Coopland, "Crime and Punishment in Paris," in *Medieval and Middle Eastern Studies in Honor of Aziz Suryal Atiya* (Leiden: E.J. Brill, 1972), 85.

38.   Ibid., 84.

39.   Jonathan Dewald, "The 'Perfect Magistrate': Parlementaires and Crime in Sixteenth-Century Rouen," *Archiv für Reformationsgeschichte/Archive for Reformation History* 67 (1976): 287.

40.   Ibid., 289, 292.

41.   Le Roy Ladurie, *The Royal French State*, 3. See also Ernst Kantorowicz, *The King's Two Bodies: A Study in Medieval Political Theology* (Princeton: Princeton University Press, 1957).

42.   Le Roy Ladurie, *The Royal French State*, 4.

43.   Ibid., 3.

44.   Gauvard, "Fear of Crime," 25.

45.   Quoted in Collins, "State Building," 618. On the absolute power of the ruler as interpreted by Bodin, see also Carl Schmitt, *Political Theology: Four Chapters on the Concept of Sovereignty* (Cambridge, Mass.: MIT Press, 1985), 8-9.

46. Hanawalt and Wallace, "Introduction," in *Medieval Crime and Social Control*, xi.
47. C. Hignett, *Xerxes' invasion of Greece* (Oxford: Clarendon Press, 1963), 64.
48. While observing Ottoman incorporation of criminals into the state, one must remember that the Ottoman empire's resort to tactics of incorporation was not only the result of a specific political culture. In many cases it was also due to weakness of the state. Karen Barkey, *Bandits and Bureaucrats: The Ottoman Route to State Centralization* (Ithaca: Cornell University Press, 1994) (page citations in text).
49. Vernadsky, *The Mongols*, 49, 44; see also Andrew Robert Burn, *Persia and the Greeks: The Defence of the West, c. 546-478 B.C.* (London: Edward Arnold, 1970), 63.

2

The Proliferation of Asocial Processes and the Problem of Control

Thus, the early modern state was conditioned in its dealing with criminals by the nature of the legalistic culture that started to emerge and define the state's approach to society. The notion of the emerging social contract in its modern Western meaning excluded the possibility of the incorporation of those increasing numbers who engaged in asocial behavior. The flexibility of the king in this case was quite limited. But this was not the only problem of the state in the early modern era. Asocial processes were often of such a nature that they precluded "domestication" through incorporation even if the royal power chose to do this. The king could "forgive" the noble who together with a small army, engaged in highway robbery. Theoretically, some nobles could even be incorporated into the elite and become part of the king's entourage. And this was done not only in the Orient (e.g., Turkey), but in France as well, at least on occasion. But the king could not "forgive" and reincorporate into society, especially into the elite part of society, the hordes of criminalized mercenaries and vagabonds who often engaged in stealing and violence. A broad application of repression was the only way of solving these problems.

In dealing with these asocial processes the state occupied a difficult position, at least at the beginning of its efforts. This was due not only to the fact that the state confronted a variety of problems, but also to other factors. The forces that strengthened the state and undermined the stability of the state and society worked at the same time.

At the beginning of the modern era the constructive forces were in a disadvantageous position, for the process of social disintegration was much stronger than the forces that led to the solidification of the bureaucratic apparatus of the state. The strength of the state came from the ability of rulers to build the modern bureaucratic apparatus and army. The strength of these institutions and the ability of rulers to use them in strengthening their power were in many ways due to the change in the relationship between rulers and the people under their command. Interpersonal relationships were in many ways replaced by the social contract. Soldiers, for example, followed the ruler mostly because they were paid. An absolutely different relationship had held people in the feudal era when the bonds that kept people together (the ruler and his warriors) were of a personal nature. They had been *Gemeinschaft* ties.

Contractual obligation became possible because of the introduction of money into social relationships. However, while money and money-based relationships made the creation of the state apparatus possible, they aided the erosion of the family style structures that had been the foundation of medieval life. These same forces unleashed legions of predatory mercenaries, gangs of vagabonds, and similar folk. Moreover, the combination of political, social, and biological calamities hastened the process of disintegration. Although the resources of the state and the strength of the apparatus increased over time, the range of calamities increased even faster. The agents of the European states knew that they needed to weed out antisocial aspects of life and that the major way to accomplish this goal was with control and repression. Yet they did not have enough resources to deal with all problems and needed to prioritize.

While choosing the most important problems to deal with, authorities usually had several criteria in mind. To start with there was the type of crime. Each judicial system had its own priorities. Topping the list were the most dangerous types of crimes, those that involved weapons and violence and threatened the existence of society. Most dangerous were the armed bandits that constituted the armed forces. They could control an entire region and make it quasi-independent from the central regime. Banditry could sever the communication between regions of the country. Homicide was also regarded as a very serious crime. Murder was a flagrant attack against the king's authority. It was a breach of the essence of the contract between the king and his subjects, since one of the king's major duties was to prevent the murder of his subjects. Consequently, the central power was mostly focused on reducing these most dangerous crimes (crimes based on violence and the use of arms).

Special attention was paid to the groups most likely to create problems. These groups not only formed a breeding ground for crime, but also were numerous enough to constitute a danger to public order on a grand scale. The danger from these groups compelled the state and society to allocate precious, limited repressive resources to deal with them. It was also impossible to cover the entire country with equal vigilance. For this reason the major concerns were the most politically/socially sensitive areas. They included the capitals, the residence of the monarch, big cities, and major roads. The other parts of the country were comparatively marginalized in case of pressing problems in these vital areas.

The emerging centralized state not only prioritized its actions against various manifestations of asocial behavior but also developed means of dealing with pressing asocial problems. In designing ways of dealing with these problems, agents of the state took into consideration the facts that the resources at their disposal were limited, the judicial system was not strongly developed, and the central government had few agents at its disposal. This complicated the task of finding criminals, and many escaped punishment. At the same time, the acuteness of the problems required a radical solution. These conditions certainly constrained the means the centralized authorities used to deal with criminal behavior.

These finally boiled down to two basic types of actions, both strongly resemble actions implemented on a grand scale by totalitarian regimes. First was the rejection of the "presumption of innocence." Individuals who belonged to dangerous groups, which were seen as hotbeds of criminal activity, were regarded as guilty by definition of belonging to these groups. This was the case with vagabonds, beggars, and similar folk. They were to be apprehended and isolated en masse without consideration of individual guilt or lack thereof.

Second was the practice of "arbitrariness of punishment" in general. The law provided only the general outline of the method of punishment. Actual application depended exclusively on the personal preference of the judges, especially if the person committed a crime regarded as grave.

Third was the application of the death penalty on a large scale. The death penalty was primarily employed to stop uncontrolled violence such as banditry, robbery (especially armed robbery), rape, and similar crimes. Yet severe punishments could be used for a variety of crimes a judge saw as dangerous. Not only were the deaths public, but they were usually accompanied by an array of sophisticated tortures. All this was to instill potential culprits with overwhelming fear.

The graphic descriptions of the sophisticated and brutal punishment of criminals found in contemporary records both was a manifestation of the power of the king as a symbol of the state and had utilitarian ends. The state was unable to apprehend all criminals, and policing was unsophisticated. For this reason, the state needed to be exceptionally brutal and public in displaying cruelty in order to stop criminality. The most terrifying punishment was seen as essential to prevent state and society from lapsing into a Hobbesian "war of all against all." At least, this was the view of the majority of jurists and political thinkers.

A deep transformation of European society caused this increase of the state's hold over subjects. In the process of fighting the rising asocial processes, emerging European nations strengthened their institutions of control and repression, through the institutions of bureaucracy or the emerging civil society. The law enforcement system also expanded, though slowly. The drive to discipline and punish had crucial implications for European history. The state as the major guarantor of order in the holistic sense acquired an extraordinary power that increased from the fifteenth to the seventeenth century. The increase of the king's power was not just in the fading of the power of the nobility but also in the dramatic intrusion of the state in virtually all aspects of its subjects' lives. The state became actively involved in economic activity, including property transactions. It engaged in strict regulation of sexual mores and personal activities. Its coercive/regulatory activities were often interwoven with twisted charitable/humanitarian implications. This intrusion into many aspects of human life along with the mass use of brutal violence provided the state with features often strikingly like those of totalitarian societies.

The Bringing of Order

While discussing the trend toward a more orderly society, scholars have had different ideas as to the point of departure. For both Foucault and Norbert Elias the process was in many ways due to the change of values. Of course, their evaluations of the process were different. For Foucault it led to the virtual enslavement of people in the modern West, which he lamented with a sort of postmodernist playfulness. Elias, however, regarded this as a positive conversion from uncontrolled barbarism to civilized society. We here propose a different point of departure. As demonstrated in our study, the drive against the various forms of asocial behavior was caused not only by changes in values, but also by pressing problems that undermined the very existence of society. Thus, the transition to a more orderly society was a result not so much of the internal evolution of values as of the dramatic increase of repression. Real destructive elements caused fear of various aspects of the asocial process and a craving for order and organization, not the emergence of an "episteme" unrelated to real life. These destructive aspects existed throughout the

Middle Ages and were in many respects, for example the spread of crime and disease, intensified by the beginning of the modern era.

The major engine for the push to end asocial behavior was not the result of a change in values or even of the development of institutions responsible for maintaining order, for example, the police. The law enforcement mechanism was in an embryonic stage. It developed slowly and could hardly in itself stand against the tidal wave of asocial behavior. Thus, the brutality of repression should be seen as the major engine of the change toward the normalization of society, and this brutality partially compensated for the state's lack of efficient law enforcement. The sheer brutality and its public displays provided instruction to a broad segment of the population and instilled in them respect for law and order.

The Ideology of Repression: Humans as Animals

The rulers as the embodiment of law were seen as ideal, nearly divine figures. The story was quite different for the subjects. The assumption was broadly circulated that repression was essential to rule and that humans were not much different from animals and driven by instincts.

In various forms a majority of political thinkers shared the assumption that a strong state and brutal punishment were a must. In the sixteenth and seventeenth centuries, political thought had developed a great deal, and certain structural similarities could be detected in the works of a variety of thinkers—Thomas Hobbes (1588-1679) and Niccoló Machiavelli (1469-1527) as two of the best-known cases.

Machiavelli's unflattering description of human beings might be one of the best to characterize the vision that spread among the elite: "For this may be said of men generally: they are ungrateful, fickle, feigners and dissemblers, avoiders of danger, eager for gain."[1] Even if there is an external display of real attachment, one should not be deceived, for even here was some hidden pragmatic consideration: "While you benefit them they are all devoted to you: they would shed their blood for you; they offer their possessions, their lives, and their sons, as I said before, when the need to do so is far off. But when you are hard pressed, they turn away." While seeing the human being as driven exclusively by animal instincts (fear, greed, lust, etc.), Machiavelli stated clearly that the ruler must be as unscrupulous with the people as they would be with him. For example, he could easily forget all about his promises.

Machiavelli was important, not because he was well known, but because, more than anyone else, he was the spokesman for many rulers. There is evidence of his influence on some French kings, Henri

III, for example.[2] Some kings, such as François I, while unaware of Machiavelli, still behaved in a way that could be "described as pre-Machiavellian."[3]

Hobbes, who lived after Machiavelli in the seventeenth century, had essentially the same view of humans and made the point even more bluntly. While Hobbes did not regard humans as similar to animals, due to their superior capacity for reason, he believed that reason and, implicitly, the ability to collect knowledge did not lead to a better society, as had been suggested by classical antiquity, as well as by some philosophers of the Enlightenment, especially those in the Anglo-American tradition. Indeed, those of the Anglo-American tradition considered that reason, knowledge, and education would lead to a higher moral caliber of citizen, and therefore improve societal processes.[4]

This assumption was absolutely foreign to Hobbes, who saw no relationship between reason and morality. He assumed that each particular individual saw no relationship between his interest and the interest of the rest of society and thought his gain was somebody else's loss, and vice versa. Man was driven by passionate, animalistic desire. Reason just provided him the best way to attain what he wanted. In Hobbes's view, "reason is essentially a servant of passion."[5] In this interpretation, reason made a man a cunning and brutish beast of prey, and led to the condition "where every man is the enemy of every other, endeavoring to destroy or subdue him by force or fraud or both. This is nothing but a state of war."[6] In Hobbes's view, if one employs the modern expression, humans lived under the law of the jungle. And to be sure, neither in his political design nor in that of other political thinkers from the fifteenth through sixteenth centuries, was there any discussion of broad masses of people participating in management of their affairs. In fact, thinkers tended to elaborate on the vision of Machiavelli and Hobbes that a brutal government was needed to tame the human animal.

Despite the images the Italian Renaissance produced and disseminated, images of the masses, average persons, were predominantly negative, and by the late Renaissance, especially at the time of the Counter-Reformation and beyond in the seventeenth century, these feelings increased. Even such a prominent thinker as Thomas More, the author of *Utopia* and one of the earliest proponents of a socialist society, shared Hobbes's feeling that human beings are essentially vicious and can be restrained only through force. With all their differences, the two authors saw coercion as an essential aspect of societal life. Even for More, coercion, for example, slavery for those who would sin, was seen as essential.

The rising Protestant movement also had a rather gloomy vision of humans—human flesh was weak. Protestants desired not the authorities' vigorous supervision, but also (even more so) alertness on the part of believers, who were to repress the flesh so as not to fall into the sins of the lustful and weak body. In the northern Renaissance, in the cultural output of the region where Protestantism spread, this vision of the human spread rapidly. In their vision of humans, the northern Renaissance painters were much blunter than their southern counterparts. In the paintings of Hieronymus Bosch (1450?-1516), Albrecht Dürer (1471-1528), and Pieter Brueghel (1525-1569), one sees people at best as playful animals. But in most cases, especially in Bosch's work, humans were animals driven by lust and vanity; in fact, they were worse than animals: they were perverted monsters. The power of reason, restrictive at best, did not dull human lust but simply made it worse. The fact that the human mind drove these animal behaviors made them perverse.

The depth of pessimism in regard to the essentially beastly nature of humans could be seen among such thinkers as Samuel Pufendorf (1632-1694) and Baruch Spinoza (1632-1677), who "have described man in the state of nature as 'evil,' i.e., 'like the beasts moved by their drives (hunger, cupidity, fear, jealousy).'"[7] It was not surprising in this context that there were no strong political thinkers in the sixteenth and seventeenth centuries who emphasized political freedom or slackening of control over an individual.

This above-presented information can be explained in the context of the development in political thought. A majority of observers thought that weakness of control would inevitably culminate in an outburst of a different and very destructive form of antisocial behavior. This would take many lives and cause much more destruction than the most repressive rulers. The political and judicial elite were also quite aware of the fragility of the social order. The intensity of the desire to engage in criminal behavior was very strong, and it was basically correct in its gloomy vision of the social landscape in front of them. The drive toward criminality was enmeshed in social conflict; in fact, there was great fluidity in this respect. A social outburst could easily evolve into looting; looting could take the form of popular revolt. Both types of breakdown could happen quite easily.

The societal structure was extremely fragile for several reasons. First, there was not only a gaping distance between rich and poor but also a gap between the conspicuously affluent and the semi-starving majority. In cases of famine or other economic calamities, actual starvation became a reality. "Historians tell us that France witnessed 13 nationwide famines in the sixteenth century" and that famine could be especially deadly in an unusually cold winter such as that in 1544. It was so cold that "wine had to be cut in the cask with sharp instruments."[8] These famines often drove people to desperation. One report stated that "people were 'living on grass like animals.'"[9]

Second, the hold of the legalistic religion of Western capitalism with its respect for private property as a "sacred" institution was quite weak, especially among marginal groups. Indeed, the law in its universal meaning—that is, the assumption that certain rules of societal interactions are mandatory for all members of the society—was foreign to a considerable part of the population.[10] In addition, the masses in most cases held only nebulous images of their political goals. Their riots were in most cases spontaneous responses to the gut fear of the deterioration of their economic conditions and the starvation famine entailed.[11] Violence with looting could erupt quite easily, and it was only a sign of the most terrifying punishment and the memory of such punishment that could check the crowd.[12] For these reasons, brutalization of punishment was an essential aspect of the law and basic order until the end of the ancien régime. Jurists well understood this: "Punishments alone gave force to the law and its commands; without them, there could be no empire of the law over crimes, criminals and the generality of civil society."[13]

Joseph de Maistre (1753-1821), who in his appraisal of the work of the executioner saw him as the foundation of society, as the only way of keeping members of society from falling out of society and into the world of criminality, was a good example of this viewpoint. His view was grounded in the tradition of the ancien régime. The view of a majority, or at least many judicial officials of the French ancien régime, was that the Hobbesian vision of society was correct. Society was a war of everyone against everyone, and brutal passion would tear it into pieces without appropriate checks. For this reason, the point of these thinkers was not to design a free society, but rather to find political agencies, a form of government that could restrain by brutal force a considerable part of the population, if not the majority.

Since people, human beings in general, in all these political designs emerged as brutal beasts, only a strong central power could curb them, prevent them from running amok and tearing society apart and finally perishing from what they had done. However, while there were no images of the ideal populace, there were images of the ideal ruler or elite. Although the elite could be drawn from a broad segment of society, and exactly who and what they were could be interpreted in various ways, they were distinctly set aside from the majority. Ideal humans in the portraits of Renaissance painters were not really a presentation of idealized humanity, but rather of the idealized elite, considered the best representatives of the species.

Thus, these strong authorities with their assortment of brutal punishments were recognized as being indispensable because it was felt that society could not be engaged in self-policing and, for this reason, could not survive on its own. And for these reasons, there was no opiate to create a government "for the people and by the people." As a matter of fact, the sixteenth- and seventeenth-century revolutions were not so much democratic in nature as oligarchic/autocratic revolutions. Indeed, the sixteenth through seventeenth century witnessed revolution in the Netherlands and in England. In both cases, a different sort of government replaced the monarchy. Yet William, Prince of Orange (1533-1584), leader of the "United Provinces of the Netherlands," was "hereditary *stadholder*,"[14] and Oliver Cromwell (1599-1658) was "Lord Protector," in fact a dictator. In any case it was assumed that only those with property could engage in the decision making process. Yet this emphasis on the importance of property cannot be explained in purely Marxist terms, i.e., that the state served only the interests of the proprietors and therefore wished to reduce the populace's engagement in politics. The reason was of a deeper social-religious nature. Those who owned property were not just blessed or lucky, but were those who were able to master their destructive animal drives and become productive members of society. There were few people with a substantial amount of property, so it was assumed that only a few had mastered their instincts. The majority were poor and therefore nothing but cunning animals, or at least people who could fall into the trap of their own instincts. The duty of the chosen few was to be not benign, but rather harsh shepherds over the flock of unruly beasts. Likewise, even some shepherds (read elite) could fall into the trap of sin; therefore the state should never relax its vigilant gaze and keep the sword of punishment always ready for action.

The Deployment of Terror

Simmel argues that "It is quite generally held that coercion is necessary for social organization" and "for the majority of men, coercion probably is an irreplaceable support and cohesion of the inner and outer life."[15] While coercion can be seen in any state, any social organization, including the modern Western state, direct coercion is not as decisive an element of the social/political structure of modern states, barring of course periods of social violence, that is, cases of emergency. Some observers saw such cases as a precondition for dictatorial regimes.[16] For example, Carl Schmitt defined such a situation as the time of "exception." And he provided a definition of it: "The exception, which is not codified in the existing legal order, can at best be characterized as a case of extreme peril, a danger to the existence of the state, or the like." And in other places he added, "The state suspends the law in the exception on the basis of its right of self-preservation, as one would say."[17]

Yet with all his insight, Schmitt, like most modern Westerners, could hardly comprehend the meaning of emergency in the period. His observation of the emergency situation was inevitably bound by personal experience and recent history. And all examples of recent history, in the European context, indicated that the emergency was in most cases the result of a few sets of problems. Most important to our study, these periods of danger were comparatively short. For example, during the French Revolution, the state of emergency, which some historians suggest produced the Reign of Terror, lasted only a few years. It was longer during the Nazi era when the social instability and the danger of the war justified Hitler's dictatorship. And this sense of social instability induced Schmitt to see in the dictatorship a solution to the country's problems. The Soviet regime retained a state of instability and perceived mortal threat (at least in the mind of the Soviet officials) for a much longer period, one of several generations. Yet by Brezhnev's era, it had acquired a sense of stability and security. One might argue that this sense of security induced Gorbachev to slacken control over society, which eventually led to the regime's demise.[18]

In modern European history, states of emergency have been rather limited, and dictatorial or terrorist regimes could not indefinitely appeal to the situation of emergency as justification for their repressive policies. This, however, was not the case in late medieval/early modern Europe, where the state was always in a position of emergency. It could not relax. Mortal danger was everywhere and criminality, in various forms, especially if it was connected to the application of violence, could easily undo not only the state but also society. The apparatus of repression was weak, in the process of creation. The state in such situations not only prioritized areas of the most importance for its survival but also acted with the utmost brutality.

The assumption that the ruler must be brutal was apparently widespread in fifteenth- through sixteenth-century European thought. Once again, Machiavelli is a good example. He is one of the few philosophers whose name produced an adjective, "Machiavellian," often defined as behavior characterized "by cunning duplicity and bad faith." This interpretation implies that Machiavelli was a pragmatic relativist not hobbled by any broad moral social considerations in regard to the public good, and the theory of power that he displayed in *The Prince* was a manual that instructed cunning and unprincipled politicians on how to take and maintain power at all costs. The popularity of Machiavelli among modern dictators (for example, there is evidence that Lenin had read him) certainly reinforced this vision of the theory. In these cases, their dictatorships were seen as motivated by nothing but a drive for power for its own sake. This vision was also supported by actual practice of many Italian rulers of Machiavelli's time, especially the Borgia family, with whom Machiavelli was fascinated. All the members of the family needed power for its own sake and the personal benefits that it provided.

However, instruction in achievement and maintenance of power was only one part of the Machiavellian message. According to Machiavelli, power required that the ruler concern himself with the public good. He implied that upon achieving the highest position the ruler must not be absolutely selfish, but think about the well-being of his subjects. Most important was preservation of their lives and property. For this purpose terror was indispensable.

While elaborating on the high calling that must inspire the ruler, Machiavelli revealed a strong moral underpinning. "I maintain that every ruler should want to be thought merciful, not cruel."[19] This appeal to be merciful was for more than pragmatic considerations, albeit Machiavelli assumed that such a rule would be more stable. The ruler was not a self-seeking individual but a person whose actions were conditions for the benefit of the public. However, this appeal had an additional meaning for Machiavelli. For this reason he ended the above quoted phrase with the statement that "one should take care not to be merciful in an inappropriate way." Mercy, if applied without reservation, could lead "disorders to develop, with the resulting killings and plundering." Brutal repressiveness and salutary fear were needed, not only to keep the ruler in power, but also for the benefit of society. Machiavelli added that the fear brutality would cause did not preclude love for the ruler. In fact, he implied that a fear/love relationship between ruler and subjects was a normal relationship. And here he sounded almost Orwellian. Elaborating on the importance of fear, he nevertheless stated that fear (accepted and even expected from the subjects) as an essential aspect of stability must not be mistaken for hatred. If the leader used power as arbitrary indulgence, without concern for his subjects, hatred would emerge. It also emerged when the ruler acted as a bandit rather than as a force that fought banditry. In this case, Machiavelli implied, the ruler betrayed his high calling as the leader and endangered his physical survival. No repression would guarantee the survival of the ruler or his descendants if his regime was hated. However, the populace would tolerate terrorist measures, and actually expect them, if they were used to maintain order. Terror made the power of the state even stronger when it was the means for protecting citizens from fear of foreign invasion and/or for liberation of the country from foreign threat.[20] Thus, brutality was seen as an essential aspect of rule. And while few rulers had read Machiavelli or had even heard of him, following their political instincts they actually acted according to his maxims.

From the fifteenth through sixteenth centuries, terror was broadly used to paralyze the will of potential criminals and prevent the most destructive forces from spreading. The broad use of public torture was also designed for this reason. The message that the state sent to potential criminals could be formulated as follows: The chance of apprehension is low. However, if a criminal is apprehended he or she will die in a most gruesome fashion.

Thus, one cannot see ideological drives as causing gruesome executions and the wide employment of capital punishment, despite the all-important ideology of emerging capitalism that emphasized the rigidity of the application of the law. While one must give this ideology its due, one needs to remember the purely pragmatic implication of terror. This brutality was the only way the state could maintain and slowly expand the areas of safety and order, the only way the state could slowly decrease the role of violence in private life. These considerations explained why the applications of the death penalty and the sophistication of torture techniques made such great leaps forward at the beginning of the modern era.

The death penalty and accompanying torture, mostly used against crimes that, in the view of the authorities, undermined the foundation of society and were the manifestation of libidinous destructive passions in an individual, were one of the most popular ways of punishment. Those who made and enforced the laws viewed individuals as driven by passions. They assumed that humans were nothing but cunning animals that could be stopped in their destructive activities only by fear of the most horrible punishment.

Executions were not too numerous; in fact, they were statistically negligible, at least by twentieth-century standards.[21] Yet even comparatively
few but regular executions in the major cities were more than enough to
provide a deep impact on observers. One could assume that quite a few
officials of late medieval/early modern France would subscribe to the old
Chinese proverb "Kill one to warn hundreds."[22] In late medieval/early
modern France, the impact on observers was reinforced not just by the
publicity of the executions but also by the other arrangements.

In most cases executions were accompanied by an array of sophisticated, ingenious tortures. These techniques of public execution and
mutilation of bodies were certainly not the invention of the French, nor
were they a European phenomenon. Exhibiting tortured victims in public was quite an ancient technique, widely employed both to maintain
public order and to terrify potential rebels. The bodies of the impaled,
crucified, or skinned alive were displayed on major roads and in mar-
ketplaces. Cut-off heads with popped-out eyes and protruding tongues
were displayed on poles.

Yet it seems that early modern European rulers used capital punishment much more frequently than feudal lords or even some of the oriental
despots. To understand the specificity of the early modern era and its
increasing obsession with capital punishment, often of the most macabre
type, one must remember that capital punishment was not universally
accepted as the only way for punishing the most serious crimes, even in
ancient times. This could be seen even among oriental despots who were
supposedly at ease with disposing of human life. The ancient Persian
monarchy could serve as an example. If one trusts Herodotus, the law/tra-
dition was rather cautious in application of the death sentence, and "not
even the king can execute anyone who has been accused of only a single
crime."[23] Not just free Persians, but even slaves, had a sort of protection
against arbitrary executions. "Nor can any other Persian do irreversible
harm to any of his house-slaves for committing a single crime."

The above-presented information does not imply that capital punishment was not part of the legalistic culture of ancient times, but shows
that it was not as rigorously exercised as one would assume.

At the same time, both the Dark Ages and the classical Middle Ages
were marked by rather sparing use of capital punishment. Capital punishment had been known in France since the Middle Ages, and execution
was on the records as a form of punishment for the gravest crimes since
the twelfth century, at least in d'Abbeville.[24] However, both and royal and
especially seigneurial courts were comparatively lenient. The seigneurial

courts, the major mechanism of law enforcement in the Middle Ages, continued to be comparatively lenient even at the beginning of the modern era. "Death sentences in the seigneurial courts were relatively rare and only carried out after consultation with royal officers of justice."[25] Local courts were seen to be usually more lenient than direct royal justice in the fifteenth through sixteenth century.[26] In the thirteenth century, a murderer could be merely expelled from the city.[27] During the same time period, the royal court was in fact also comparatively lenient. The last Capetian kings dealt leniently even with open rebellion and treason, phenomena that directly undermined the foundations of royal power.[28]

Capital punishment was rare not only in the West, but in early medieval Eastern Europe as well. In Kievan Russia it did not exist at all, at least in law.[29] One could find restraint even in the judicial practice of Mongols, who could hardly be accused of liberalism. Capital punishment played an important role in Mongol judicial practice, but its application was limited. Murderers, for example, were not executed, but paid fines.[30]

The beginning of the modern era led to a dramatic change in this respect: "The new emphasis upon punishment per se resulted in the regular appearance of all sorts of corporal punishments in European criminal codes. Within a brief period corporal punishment became the common form of penalty, whereas they had been exceptional penalties under the feudal system. Banishment and fines became less important aspects of the new statutes. Flogging, mutilation, and even execution were commonly prescribed for felonies; in some criminal codes, not a single felony was exempted from some form of corporal punishment. Public executions became frequent, and persons sentenced to the gallows sometimes numbered half of all those convicted of serious crimes. Various new forms of corporal punishment were introduced and, in particular, torture became commonplace in most judicial proceeding."[31] Even if one accepted the notion that in part of the region monetary punishments prevailed in the fourteenth century, the most serious crimes (e.g., homicides) were punished by death.[32] By way of comparison, one should note that in the Middle Ages homicides could be punished by fines.

Indeed, only the dawn of the modern era led to the proliferation of capital punishment, and in describing the government punishments, Gonthier used the word "terror" with justification.[33] It was not just the application of capital punishment that had risen dramatically by the beginning of the modern era, but also the application of torture. It is true that torture also had a long history, and the art and the practice of torturous dispatch of individuals never died out completely. Yet only at the advent of the modern era did torturous death become a routine type of punishment.

These views of course were not universally shared. Some historians, such as Andrew Trout, stated that by the end of the sixteenth century torture declined in judicial procedure. He also wrote that the various royal ordinances in regard to torture must not be taken at face value. He implied that these ordinances were not actually enforced and that torture was actually reduced from application to a threat.[34]

One could hardly agree with these statements. One might assume that torture was declining, with the increasing abilities of law enforcement agencies to find the facts, as a way of extracting information from the accused, forcing them to confess and reveal the names of accomplices. Yet torture increased dramatically as a part of execution. Most executions were not just about depriving the person of life, but also designed to make his end most painful. As time progressed, torture became more and more gruesome. Its wide application was an essential aspect of the increasingly brutalizing machinery of repression. Michael R. Weisser has presented the beginning of the modern era as a period of dramatic increase in the brutality of punishment, and from this perspective, the early modern era was quite different from the Middle Ages, a time characterized by "the lack of harsh punishment."[35]

The Western machinery of punishment was a good match for any oriental state, even those supposedly famous for their brutality. There were even suggestions that Western law, for example, were more brutal than Mongol law, and Russian principalities that wanted examples of the most brutal legalistic arrangements turned not to the East but to the West.[36]

Terror against Nobles and Bandits: The Hundred Years War and Beyond

The dramatic increase in the use of the death sentence and torturous death affected all members of society. The state dispatched thousands of revolting peasants.[37] This brutal punishment was by no means limited to use against the helpless populace to maintain class domination. The rebellious populace was indeed treated harshly, especially if it was engaged in mass revolts. Still, on a daily basis royal power was more threatened by the nobles and noble-related banditry. At least this was the case during the fifteenth century, at the time of the Hundred Years War. Foreign enemies and nobles were the leading forces confronting the crown. Their political confrontation was in fact criminal activity, for defiance of the crown in most cases entailed banditry on a large scale. In future centuries, the crown would try to spare the nobles from the most brutally painful and degrading punishments. Beheading would be reserved for the most egregious of nobles. Yet in the fourteenth and fifteenth centuries, great equality prevailed, in the sense that nobles engaged in politicocriminal or purely criminal enterprises were dispatched in the same brutish, degrading way as leaders of rebellious serfs. In this case the French kings were in no way different from oriental despots or their analogues—the totalitarian rulers of modern times, like Stalin, who sent to the same death both the peasant and the member of Politburo.

In the fifteenth century, in the midst of the chaos and the domination of the "anomie" in social discourse, the behavior of the nobles engaged in plundering expeditions was in no way different from that of peasant boys engaged in the same criminal pursuit. So there was not much difference in the way they should be dispatched. After the French Revolution it was decided that all citizens of the French Republic must be executed by the guillotine, the method of decapitation once reserved exclusively for nobles.

Fifteenth-century France rulers also believed in equality in executions. The difference, of course, was that they assumed commoners and nobles must suffer similar tortures and degrading death if the nature of the crime required such treatment. The wide application of torture in dealing with nobles shows clearly that in general the royal repressive/judicial machinery had little social bias and approached all members of society with equal ferocity. From this perspective one could hardly agree with Geremek's statement, elaborating on the state social bias, that "The judicial system and police apparatus were directed, first and foremost, against the lower rungs of the social hierarchy; it was they who needed to be watched, who were dangerous, who were constantly on the verge of crime."[38] Geremek in a way contradicted his own statement by acknowledging that "Contemporary literature gives us a picture of crime socially limited to the dominant classes."

Kings assumed treason to be the most serious crime, to be treated in a harsh and spectacular way. The crime of the traitor must "be clearly distinguished from that of the felons by the additional penalties of drawing and/or quartering."[39] This especially torturous execution was practiced from the beginning of the fourteenth century, when even the nobility of the highest rank could suffer such a degrading death. In the seventeenth century, it would be used only against commoners engaged in a variety of the most heinous common crimes.

The definition of treason was broad and allowed the royal power to employ torturous death in dealing with all varieties of crime. Many crimes defined as treason were common crimes such as banditry. Revolt against the king and helping his enemies was in many cases reduced to robbery and the plunder of those who were nominally under the king's protection. The so-called "private wars" were actually nothing but banditry. Dubbing these activities treason provided the justification for dealing with these individuals and their families in the most brutal way.

Nobles engaged in the "private wars"—banditry and displeasing the king in other ways—were not just beheaded, but also drawn (148).[40] The same assortment of brutal and degrading punishments awaited those who were involved in treason in the more narrow meaning of the word. "The execution in 1323 of Jourdain de l'Isle-Jourdain, Lord of Casaubon, who was stripped naked, drawn on a hurdle from the Chatelet to the gibbet, and hanged there, left a vivid impression on a contemporary chronicler" (116). The highly positioned Louis de Courcelles was tried in the 1450s: "The king's proctor demanded that he be drawn, decapitated, quartered 'as is customary' and hanged" (117). The king was apparently quite happy to follow the court recommendations. The authorities were upset if the court did not condemn the nobles to the most torturous and degrading punishment. This was the case with Louis de Luxembourg, accused of treason in 1475. "And although the *Parlement* of Paris in December 1475 condemned Louis de Luxembourg only to be decapitated, it had declared that 'given the enormity of these great and execrable crimes of lèse-majesté ... he should be quartered'" (116).

In some cases execution for important political crimes was not only exceptionally brutal, but also exceptionally degrading. This was the case with "would-be poisoner Jean Hardi" (117). He "suffered perhaps the most severe punishment in the reign of Louis XI. On 31 March 1474 he was 'drawn on hurdle from (the Conciergerie) to the gate of (the Louvre), and from there taken in a tumbrel to the Place de Greve, where he was 'decapitated (and) quartered. His head (was then impaled) on the end of a lance, and each of his four limbs was taken to the four towns closest to the extremities of the kingdom.' His dismembered corpse was then burned, reduced to ashes and scattered to the wind" (117-18). Those who made direct attacks on the king and the institution of the state suffered the most gruesome types of death. The wrong word could be enough; Simon Pouillet was "executed for having indiscreetly said in public that Edward III rather than Philippe de Valois should be king of France" (117). For this indiscretion, he suffered one of the first cases of quartering. The contemporary chronicle depicted his death in a rather colorful way: "'Like a side of meat in a butcher shop' he was 'stretched and bound on a slab of wood...and was there beheaded and dismembered, first his arms, then his legs, and then his head; and finally (his corpse) was hanged on the gibbet.'"

Cases of "treason" were interpreted broadly and provided the king the opportunity for harsh punishment of nobles who engaged in banditry. As a matter of fact, banditry was directly connected to treason. One manifestation of treason was the ravaging and killing of the king's subjects. The royal power started to deal with banditry as treason cases, with utmost brutality. This was the case with Charles VII. "In Champagne in 1441 he had an example made of Alexandre, bastard of Bourbon, who had been involved in the revolts of his brother of the duke in 1437 and 1440" (197). The acts of treason had apparently involved not just fighting against the king, but also rape, looting, and murder of the king's subjects. Alexandre was apprehended by royal justice and was to suffer a painful and most humiliating type of death. "Tried by summary court martial on the king's orders, he was tied in a sack and drowned in the Aube. That and twenty other executions got the message across, for leaders of rowdier bands in the region lost no time in making their submission" (197).

Similarly tough treatment was imposed on a band of Coquillards, an important group in the fifteenth-century French history, not only because of its size, "it is estimated that the whole company numbered 500 or even 1,000 brigands,"[41] but also because some nobles played a role in the band. Included in its ranks were prominent people such as Villon. The band "devastated Burgundy," but was finally routed by the authorities and fifteen members of the band "finished up on the gibbet." Even more important for the authorities was the fact that "one of them, to save his head, betrayed the customs of the company, its secret language, and the names of its leaders." This certainly helped the authorities.

The most radical extermination of those who endangered the king's power did not leave the members of the family intact. The principle of collective guilt was still alive. Shortly after a certain Jean de la Roche-Tesson was executed in April 1344, his wife petitioned the king, arguing that "according to written law a married woman ought not to lose her dowry because of the crime of her husband, be it for treason or otherwise."[42] The woman humbly added that she needed the money not just for herself, but also for her young children.

While reading her petition, one can recall the famous expression of Stalin that "children are not responsible for their fathers," that is, that the children of an "enemy of the people" could be well be good Soviet citizens. Stalin did not shoot the children of his enemies. This was not the case with wives of "enemies of the people." They were either dispatched together with their husbands or sent to the camps. The response of the French kings to the plight of those who regarded as the king's enemies was in a way similar to that of Stalin. The king, Philippe VI in this case, did not respond positively to her request, and the property was confiscated. One might add that Philippe VI acted in accordance with existing tradition (120-21). In the above case the woman, while deprived of her property, was not personally molested. Yet this did not mean that fourteenth- and fifteenth-century practices were cardinally different from those in Stalinist USSR. In direct rebellion, in the heat of battle, the slaughter was total and the wives and children shared the fate of the head of the family. Cuttler implied that even noble women were not immune from being burned at the stake (118).

The king used harsh punishment for liquidation of nobles who engaged in the most serious crimes and also for purifying the bureaucracy. In pre-modern practice embezzlement was often institutionalized in order to create a reliable apparatus for governing. Repression was used by the state against this malady. In some cases the crown fined the accused. The fine could be "enormous," something no one could pay (119). Those who could not pay received further punishment. In other cases, a painful and degrading death sentence was the immediate response to abusing the king's trust. In some cases the victim's attempt to prolong his life led to even more pain and ignominy. "In April 1328 Pierre Remi, chief treasurer of the late Charles IV, was sentenced to be hanged for maladministration. Just as he was about to be executed he admitted 'that he had committed treason against the king and the kingdom in Gascony.' Because of his confession he was immediately taken down from the gibbet, 'tied to the tail of the four-horse chariot that had transported him (there), drawn from (that gibbet) to the new (one), which he himself had caused to be built, and was the first one to be hanged there" (116-17). High royal bureaucrats who abused their power and the trust of the autocrat were treated the same rough way. Guillaume Mariette, who had been a part of the Dauphin's household, was accused of forging the royal seal and other criminal undertakings. He confessed under torture and was duly quartered (204).

In repression against the nobles the king did not always look for the really guilty. The accusation of various crimes was often just an excuse for eliminating the politically dangerous. Additional incentives could also be a chance to confiscate the money of the nobles. The executions of the wealthy and powerful were also often a good public campaign; these purges demonstrated to the populace that no one was above the law. While the legalistic culture was reinforced in such a twisted way, it benefited the king's image from another perspective. The populace was usually pleased to see a powerful person end life in the most miserable way. The king's justice mimicked the vengeance of the gods, who, the Greeks thought, did not like those who were too powerful and mighty. This gave the king the image of defender of the populace against the abusive, wealthy elite who had become fat at the people's expense.

This practice too was widespread both in the past and in modern times. Stalin often purged the bureaucracy with the excuse of purification of moral degeneration and common crime—corruption, stealing state funds, etc. The fact was that a great segment of the bureaucracy were guilty of these crimes.[43] Since the early modern French bureaucracy had many more opportunities to abuse power for personal benefit than the Soviet bureaucracy did, the kings could easily frame bureaucrats for such crimes whenever they chose to do so.[44]

Several examples can illustrate the point. Jacques Coeur (ca.1395-1456) was a financier of Charles VII. "He was an extra-ordinary man, 'a brilliant emulator of the Italian businessmen of his time' and the great servant to the king."[45] It seems that his contribution to the prosperity of the kingdom was considerable, including a huge loan to the crown that enabled the king "to reconquer Normandy" and restore the soundness of the kingdom's finances. But the wealth and influence acquired through involvement in the royal business probably created feelings of jealousy and suspicion in the king, or at least in those who were close to him. The chance to confiscate the man's fortune was possibly an additional incentive to get rid of him. Coeur was accused of poisoning Agnes Sorel, the "Dame de Beauté," the chief royal mistress. Under this accusation, "he was thrown into prison in 1451 and a trial prepared."[46] Unlike Stalin's henchmen, the king did not need to resort to psychological pressure—depriving the accused of sleep—or simple orders to beat him. The judicial machinery had at its disposal an array of sophisticated tortures, and Coeur would most likely have succumbed to pressure, accepting guilt for everything. "Fortunate for him, he escaped, dying in 1456 in Cyprus, in the service of the Pope." This case was far from isolated. "A similar but more tragic lot befell Jacques de Beaune, Baron de Semblancay (1445-1527), one of the family of merchant bankers from Touraine, where the frequent visits by king of France had led to a number of local fortunes being made." Beaune had served several kings, and finally became the chief financier of François I. His wealth and influence apparently created quite a few enemies, yet he was confident enough in his own power to dare not to provide funding for the king's disastrous Italian expedition. While the king was in captivity, his enemies had him arrested. He was condemned to death and duly "hanged on the gibbet at Montfaucon." The hanging was not only painful, but also a humiliating death. In some other cases the punishment did not end the person's life, but involved painful mutilation. For example, one's eyes could be "gouged out."[47] Here, Cuttler implied that these punishments could be applied to nobles.

As the treatment of nobles for crimes such as treason differed little from that of commoners, the same could also be said about the other privileged estate, the clergy. Since the Middle Ages the clergy had claimed immunity from the punishments of civilian authority. The power of the church and weakness of the state provided powerful backing for the claim. The state hardly accepted these notions, and from the thirteenth century there were cases when the authorities ignored the protests of the church. The authorities justified doing so by the fact that quite a few people falsely claimed clergy status.[48] Broad interpretation of treason provided the king the opportunity to persecute all groups of the population, including clerics who otherwise claimed judicial immunity.[49] With the decline of the power of the church as a universal, transnational organization, and the rise of the national state, this immunity was ignored in increasing numbers of cases. And similar to the gentry, the clergy could be executed in the most painful way; in some cases they were drawn.[50]

By the sixteenth century, the state tried to limit applying torturous death to people of noble origin. In most cases they were beheaded unless the nature of the crime dishonored the person, for example engaging in pick-pocketing. This comparative moderation could possibly be explained by the fact that the royal power already felt itself more secure than before. Still, in the case of the most dangerous political crimes, torture and degrading death could be applied to the nobles as well.

For some of the most serious crimes, the victim could undergo such exotic and painful executions as being torn apart by horses. The victim was attached to two different horses mounted by riders, who drove the horses in opposite directions and actually tore the victim apart. This method of execution was performed on Poltrot de Mere, who had assassinated the Duc de Guise, "the leader of the Catholic party."[51] Contemporary pictures illustrate the entire procedure. The victim was tied to four different mounted horses that moved in different directions. While the procedure caused the victim excruciating pain by dislocating his joints and muscles, it was not able to tear him apart as was apparently desired by the executioner. For this reason, the executioner slashed the stretched body with a sword so as to help the horses tear the victim.

Despite the gruesomeness of French punishments, they were not the worst cases. One need not travel to Asia or to Russia to see even more exquisite tortures and ways of executions.[52] One need only to cross the Channel. Cuttler, while elaborating on the array of French punishments, added that they were more humane than English ones, and that there were no "disemboweling and burning of entrails as in England."[53] If rebellious and essentially criminalized nobles were treated brutally, their retinue/mercenaries were decimated without ado. This was seen as the only way to treat them. Machiavelli, for example, praised ancient military leaders who, by applying extreme cruelty, prevented the spread of bandits/soldiers and maintained the discipline of the troops.[54]

Notes

1.   Machiavelli, *The Prince*, 59.
2.   Edmund H. Dickerman, "Henry III of France: Student of the Prince," *Bibliothèque d'Humanisme et Renaissance: Travaux et Documents* 40, 2 (1978).
3.   Le Roy Ladurie, *The Royal French State*, 57.
4.   One might assume that one reason for state support of educational institutions (e.g., colleges and universities) was the assumption that education led to better citizenship.
5.   Parsons, *The Structure of Social Action*, 89.
6.   Ibid., 90.
7.   Strauss, "Comments on Carl Schmitt's *Der Begriff des Politischen*," 96.
8.   Fernand Braudel, *The Identity of France*, 2 vols. (New York: HarperCollins, 1986-1990), 2: 384, 245.
9.   Ibid., 383.
10.   This assumption about the universal validity of law provided the framework for the judicial machinery in the modern West and is a major reason Western capitalist states need comparatively weak repressive machinery. Characterizing this culture, Simmel stated: "Legal conflict rests on a broad basis of unities and agreements between the enemies. The reason is that both parties are equally subordinated to the law; they mutually recognize that the decision is to be made only according to the objective weight of their claims." Simmel, *On Individuality*, 85.
11.   Braudel, *The Identity of France*, 2: 386.
12.   Ibid., 363, 382.
13.   Richard Andrews, "The Death Penalty in Old Regime France," in *Perspectives on Punishment: An Interdisciplinary Exploration*, ed. Richard M. Andrews (New York: Peter Lang, 1997), 68.
14.   "William I," *Encyclopedia Britannica Online*.
15.   Simmel, *On Individuality*, 343, 344.
16.   Carl Schmitt, *Political Theology: Four Chapters on the Concept of Sovereignty* (Cambridge, MA: MIT Press, 1985), 5.
17.   Ibid., 6, 12.

18. Vladimir Shlapentokh, *Normal Totalitarian Society: How the Soviet Union Functioned and How It Collapsed* (Armonk, NY: M.E. Sharpe, 2001).
19. Machiavelli, *The Prince*, 58.
20. See also Vernadsky, *The Mongols*, 344, 358, 396.
21. Gauvard, *"De grace especial"*, 897.
22. Craig S. Smith, "China's Efforts Against Crime Make No Dent," *New York Times on the Web*, 26 December 2001.
23. Herodotus, *The Histories* (Oxford: Oxford University Press, 1988), 62.
24. Jean Boca, *La justice criminelle de l'échevinage d'Abbeville au moyen-âge, 1184-1516* (Lille: Imprimerie L. Dansel, 1930), 215.
25. David Potter, "'Rigueur de justice': Crime, Murder and the Law in Picardy, Fifteenth to Sixteenth Centuries," *French History* 11, 3 (1997): 269.
26. Ibid., 274.
27. Boca, *La justice criminelle*, 196.
28. Cuttler, *The Law*, 142 (citations in text).
29. Vernadsky, *The Mongols*, 363.
30. Ibid., 113.
31. Michael Weisser, *Crime and Punishment in Early Modern Europe* (Atlantic Highlands: Humanities Press, 1979), 101.
32. Jacques Chiffoleau, *Les justices du pape: délinquance et criminalité dans la région d'Avignon au quatorzième siècle* (Paris: Publications de la Sorbonne, 1984), 215, 214, 216.
33. Gonthier, *Délinquance*, 250, 268.
34. Andrew Trout, *City on the Seine: Paris in the Time of Richelieu and Louis XIV* (New York: St. Martin's Press, 1996), 86.
35. Weisser, *Crime and Punishment*, 100. The assumption about the rareness of capital punishment in Europe, France in particular, is questioned by some historians. Maurice Bauchond stated that the death sentence was used quite often in the Middle Ages. The problem is that historians have regarded the end of the fourteenth and even the fifteenth century as the Middle Ages. Actually, at the dawn of the early modern era capital punishment started to be used on a broad basis.
36. Vernadsky, *The Mongols*, 364.
37. Braudel, *The Identity*, 2: 385.
38. Bronisław Geremek, *The Margins of Society in Medieval Paris* (Cambridge: Cambridge University Press, 1987), 14.
39. Cuttler, *The Law*, 116.
40. In some cases there was a sign of humanism of a sort, which implied that a noble could be just beheaded instead of ending his life in the most painful and degrading way (227).
41. Geremek, *The Margins*, 127.
42. Cuttler, *The Law*, 120.
43. Vladimir Brovkin, *Russia After Lenin: Politics, Culture and Society* (London: Routledge, 1998).
44. The Soviet bureaucracy had economic and political limits to opportunities for stealing, but this was not the case with the post-Soviet elite. One could assume that their drive for stealing and shady deals was comparable to and even exceeded similar drives in early modern France.
45. Braudel, *The Identity*, 2: 637.
46. Ibid., 638.
47. Cuttler, *The Law*, 118.
48. Boca, *La justice*, 64.

49.   Cuttler, *The Law*, 73-75.
50.   Braudel, *The Identity*, 2: 118.
51.   Arlette Lebigre, "Quand la torture osait dire son nom," *L'Histoire* 67 (1984): 11.
52.   In some Asian nations, these gruesome ways of execution have survived to the present. In Afghanistan, both the Taliban and their rivals widely use various macabre ways of dispatching individuals, such as tearing them apart, not with horses, but with tanks, or using tanks to crush them. Marina Tsvetkova, "Taliby byli ni pri chem," *Gazeta Ru*, March 1, 2002; Eduard Babazade, "Boroda v kerosinovoi lampe," *Moskovskii Komsomolets*, May 14, 1999.
53.   Cuttler, *The Law*, 118.
54.   Machiavelli, *The Prince*, 60.

3

The Proliferation and Brutalization of Repression:
Fifteenth and Sixteenth Centuries

While the first increase in brutal punishment could be seen in the fourteenth and fifteenth centuries, the trend increased by the sixteenth century. This increasing application of brutal punishment in dealing with crime was caused not so much by the increasing brutality of the state as by its increasing desire to eliminate the most violent crimes. This desire went along with the deep transformation of the legalistic culture that moved to the forefront by the sixteenth century.

In the Middle Ages, crime, including crime that involved bodily injury and death, was a private affair. Private individuals often handled the matter themselves, by fines or blood revenge,. However, "The ordinance on crime of 1570 formulated the idea that crime was not just a personal problem but an affair that endangers the public order."[1] Elaborating on these changes in legal thought and in society's approach to crime, Geremek stated: "The principle of private vengeance and of individual accusation, which requires a complaint from the victim or his family for proceeding to be instituted, gives way to that of the investigation or the prosecution of crime as a public obligation."[2]

Simmel, elaborating on the reason for this transition, stated that it was not only to increase the efficiency of law enforcement (apprehension of the criminal), but also to ensure that the criminal would not be punished more that he deserved.[3] One could hardly agree with his assumption that the state's entrance into the business of finding and punishing the criminals mitigated the rigor of the punishment. The opposite actually happened.

This transformation of crime from a private affair into a concern of the entire society was one of the major reasons for the increasing repressiveness of the state at the beginning of the modern era. One historian noted it this way: "Pierre Chaunu advanced the proposition, since followed by numerous historians, that the history of criminal behavior between the early seventeenth and late eighteenth century sees a move from the primacy of acts of personal violence to that of robbery, false pretense and fraud as the main criminal problems, with attendant growth in the harshness by which violent crimes were punished."[4] This process was already in place by the end of the sixteenth century when the judicial power wished to deal with all segments of society, as well as treat them all in the harshest way in cases involving the most serious scrims.

As time progressed, the authorities tended make punishments, including the most brutal, more impartial and also to increase the scope of terror to eradicate the most dangerous crime, especially crime that involved any form of violent behavior. The most brutal punishment was applied not to just specific groups of culprits, mostly highway bandits, politicized criminals, and leaders of the rebels, but quite broadly for all kinds of crimes. While the state applied torturous types of punishment to all types of criminals, it dealt with violence with special severity, resolving to put these activities to an end by any means possible. Consequently, the authorities reserved the most brutal executions for several major manifestations of this primordial passion.

As time progressed, the punishments became more gruesome and the death sentences more numerous, and death by torture increased widely. Some historians assumed that the numbers of death sentences were statistically negligible, but by other estimations, the death sentences had reached almost 30 percent of all cases in some localities by the end of the sixteenth century.[5] The most dangerous crimes, "which directly threatened natural and social bonds, were punished with consistent severity. Homicide was one such crime; thirty-two percent of the defendants in cases of homicide were executed, and another fifteen percent had fled and were executed in effigy."[6]

This increase in the brutality of punishments, seen from the beginning of the modern era, accelerated by the sixteenth century. Indeed by the end of the sixteenth century, the system of repression intensified. And the authorities were instructed to eradicate crime "without pity" as a direct response to the social breakdown caused by the civil war.[7] This increase in the brutality of punishment could even be seen in the actions of the papal power in Avignon, which, like the royal power, willingly sent people to execution and torture.[8]

The social/political breakdown in the fourteenth to seventeenth centuries was just one cause for this increase. While the state wanted to establish order, it had a comparatively weak law enforcement system. "Harshness of repression is normally an indication of the weakness in practice of state machinery."[9] Perhaps the importance of the executions lay not in their sheer numbers but in other aspects. Punishments became increasingly arbitrary, breaking not just with medieval custom, but also with the legal culture developing by the end of the Middle Ages. Judicial practice, despite its trappings of due process, became surprisingly similar to what the Revolutionary Tribunals both the French and Russian Revolutions practiced. During the terror of the full-fledged totalitarian regimes, for example during Stalin's purge trial, this practice would be even more common. The nature of the treason trial was that it did not require actual evidence, especially if the king expressed his desire to see the accused dispatched. Practically any action (the numbers rose over time) could be seen as treasonable. "Charles V cast his net far and wide in the prosecution of treason," and, "In the hands of Louis XI the law of treason was devastating."[10] Using the accusation of treason for terrorizing this or that segment of the population would continue as an essential aspect of repressive machinery for centuries to come. The fear of being seen as an "enemy of the king," and thus a traitor, had important implications, due to the longevity of the principle.

In the beginning, the law of treason provided justification for the principle of "arbitrariness of punishment," mostly in dealing with the nobles. The principle of arbitrariness of repression expanded, and by the fifteenth and sixteenth centuries arbitrary punishments became widely used in dealing with a variety of crimes. This terror was even more intense than in the Stalinist USSR, where terror, though intense, lasted only a generation or so.

As noted earlier, by the fifteenth and sixteenth centuries, the law provided only a general outline for judges' activities. In his decision, the judge was to be guided mainly by "his consciousness" and had in some cases almost absolute freedom in the infliction of punishment, including death.[11] One reason for such an approach was that the judicial practice was "in fact free judicial evaluation of the evidence although not described as such."[12]

While the principle of the arbitrariness of punishment was institutionalized even in eighteenth-century absolutist France, it was even more important in earlier periods when the state and the society were in the greatest danger. "It was in the course of XVI century when the adage 'all punishments were arbitrary' was accepted without doubt in French judicial doctrine."[13] The principle of arbitrary punishment is foreign to present day judicial procedure with its emphasis on the right of the accused and the importance of clear evidence of guilt. And the principle was in many ways foreign to medieval practice that rested on the Roman canon. The application of the Roman canon in medieval times was intended to restrain the essentially arbitrary punishment of the Dark Ages. "In place of the ordeals that purported to invoke the judgment of God, the Roman-canon procedure legitimated fact-finding and adjudication by public officials, judges."[14] Arbitrary punishment in many ways eliminated an essential aspect of judgment—that conviction must be based on evidence, and punishment be according to the spirit and letter of the law.

This arbitrariness was first applied in dealing with crimes that could be regarded as treasonable during the fourteenth century.[15] The principle was upheld more and more as time unfolded, and by the seventeenth century it was very popular,[16] especially in the case of gross offenses, such as sacrilege. This provided judges the ability to break with medieval traditions and customs, along with great flexibility in interpretation of the law, especially if they believed that exemplary punishment was needed for certain grave crimes.[17] But judges could not be absolutely free from the stipulations of the law; by the sixteenth century, the death sentence needed the approval of the royal judge, "a rule that in effect transferred a wide range of offences to the purview of the royal courts."[18] These judicial provisions hardly eased the harshness of the punishment or the arbitrariness with which the judicial machinery applied it.

One could also assume that the principle of arbitrariness of punishment tended to spread during the sixteenth century. While originally it was only applied to the gravest offenses, such as high treason, by the sixteenth century even the treatment of vagabonds was often relegated to the arbitrariness of the judges.[19] This stress on the "consciousness" rather than the spirit and letter of the law could well perplex modern Western lawyers. Yet the participants in the revolutionary tribunals during both the French and Russian Revolution easily understood it, as in fact did any judge in totalitarian societies of the Soviet type.

Another aspect of the death penalty was its increasing brutality. Interrogations and executions were done in the most brutal, torturous way. Simple execution was rather rare. Decapitation, for example, was reserved only for the nobility and only then when the nature of their crime did not require a death that was both torturous and degrading. Sentences were carried out in public, often accompanied by an array of frightful tortures.

The person who was going to be executed also suffered from torture while awaiting execution. It was both spiritual and physical anguish, for the prison was often awful.[20] Moreover, the public mutilation of the bodies of the condemned was not just an abstract manifestation of the power of the autocrat. Public torture had practical implications; it terrified potential criminals and served as a powerful deterrent. The educational aspects of a torturous death, the perpetual terror, the continuous display of torn and deformed flesh, were essential for the creation of basic order.

Torture was definitely not invented in France, nor was it a unique attribute of the early modern judicial system. "From the late Middle Ages and throughout the ancien régime, torture was an incident of the legal systems of all great states of continental Europe. Torture was part of the ordinary criminal procedure, regularly employed to investigate and prosecute routine crime before the ordinary courts. The system was one of judicial torture."[21] By the fifteenth century torture was "well established in fifteenth-century France."[22]

Torture began to be employed against the most serious criminals in the fourteenth century.[23] By the fifteenth century it had developed as the routine technique for interrogation or to dispatch the person in the most gruesome way. *Procédure extraordinaire* was usually applied to people engaged in the most serious crimes; the information obtained by confession was important. "The standard method seems to have been some combination of the rack and the pouring of water down the throat of the accused, though there was always room for innovation: Miquelot Fauvel, the messenger of Saint-Pol and Nemours in the 1470s, was tortured by tongs—presumably red-hot—applied to his heels."[24]

Torture "definitively became a part of criminal justice in 1539."[25] In the sixteenth century it was broadly used, for example, in the case of a "grand criminel," but with limitations—not against nobles, clerics, women, and children.[26] The sixteenth century, with its numerous disasters and the proliferation of crime, was nevertheless more secure than the fifteenth. Social differentiation affected methods of punishment, the assumption being that nobles should in most cases end life in a way different from commoners. Whereas commoners could be hanged, the nobles should be in most cases be beheaded. This punishment was regarded not only as less painful, but also as "honorable." But numerous exceptions could question the assumption that the sixteenth century was less "egalitarian" in regard to the application of torturous deaths.

According to the law, "the courts could not invent novel punishments."[27] But juries and executioners hardly were restrained in their activities. Punishment was not actually limited to the set patterns; there were a variety of execution techniques. Their origins were diverse. Some had been invented long ago, some were comparatively recently imported from other countries and were, from this point of view, cultural exchange like new literary styles, cuisines, fashions of dress, or ways of lovemaking.[28] As the art of lovemaking could well travel from one culture to another, the same could be said about ways of dispatching people. It is quite possible that knowledge of the techniques of torture and torturous death could be transmitted by merchants, scholars, diplomats, or occasional travelers who might observe executions with the same excitement and marvel with which they saw rituals, pictures, pageantry, or strange attire. Whatever their origin, they were all perfected and broadly used. Almost every type of crime had a corresponding type of torture or torturous death. Judges could easily choose "among the ghastly variety that tradition bequeathed to them."[29] Law enforcement acquired a menu of gruesome punishments.

The menu expanded as time progressed. Nicole Gonthier stated that by the fifteenth and sixteenth centuries royal power saw the death penalty as the final deterrent, and that strangulation and hanging were the most popular ways of execution by the beginning of the sixteenth century. One might think that these forms were brutal enough, but the French authority thought differently. In 1534 a royal decree introduced execution on the wheel.[30] By the seventeenth century the state had at its disposal all types of brutal punishment.

By the end of the seventeenth century, varieties of punishment were codified and rearranged in the judicial display. Physical tortures played an important role. "The ordinance of 1670 regulated the general forms of penal practice up to the Revolution. It laid down the following hierarchy of penalties: 'Death, judicial torture pending proof, penal servitude, flogging, *amende honorable*, banishment.'"[31] By that time they could be compared with those by police of the totalitarian states of the twentieth century such as the Gestapo.[32] "Capital punishment comprises many kinds of death: some prisoners may be condemned to be hanged, others to having their hands cut off or their tongue cut out or pierced and then to be hanged, others, for more serious crimes, to be broken alive and die on the wheel, after having their limbs broken; others to be broken until they die a natural death, others to be burned alive, others to be burned after first being strangled; others to be drawn by four horses, others to have their heads cut off, and others to have their heads broken."[33] Some processes were quite sophisticated, and judicial thought continued to invent new types of torture with a sort of poetic inspiration. New ways of dispatching regicides were proposed by the anonymous author of the brochure, *Hanging Not Punishment Enough* (1701). According to the proposed procedure, "the condemned man was dragged along on a hurdle (to prevent his head from smashing against the cobblestones), in which his belly was opened up, his entrails quickly ripped out, so that he had time to see them, with his own eyes, being thrown on the fire; in which he was finally decapitated and his body quartered." "The reduction of these 'thousand deaths' to strict capital punishment defines a whole new morality concerning the act of punishing." [34]

The increasing emphasis on a variety of brutal punishments was incorporated into the general spread of the sadistic enjoyment of cruelty. Not only the culture of the underworld and the variety of "anomies" that swarmed in fourteenth- through sixteenth-century France enjoyed cruelty. The culture of sadistic pleasure was actively promoted by the state itself. These could be seen in such city amusements as burning cats. Elias saw this case as the most appalling because it demonstrated "any excuse before reason,"[35] along with deeply ingrained brutality and streaks of sheer sadism in the repressive machinery of the state. Elias rightfully connected this case to the torturous executions of criminals and heretics.

The Application of the Death Penalty as the Drive against Criminality

During the Hundred Years War, sophisticated torturous death was mostly employed for the elite. This was not because the state was more brutal toward the criminalized nobility than toward the simple folk. Peasant uprisings such as the Jacquerie posed a considerable danger to the feudal class in general, and there was no doubt that rebellious peasants were dispatched in a quite brutal way.[36] It also did not mean that ordinary crimes were treated lightly. Still, the major problem of the fourteenth and fifteenth centuries, aside from foreign threats, was banditry and politicized banditry in which nobles and their retinues and soldiers were the major culprits. State resources were limited and the elaborate tortures and deaths were quite expensive.

By the sixteenth century or so, the state became more and more concerned with weeding out common crime. As time progressed and the danger from banditry became less acute, the state could shift more attention to ordinary crimes and treat them with same sadistic severity as the earlier rebellious nobles. As in the previous century, the state prioritized the most dangerous crimes, those that shook the foundation of the state and society.

The danger for the state included a variety of threats. These included several manifestations of what could be called class conflicts—uprisings of peasants and lower classes in the cities. Yet, upon the end of the Jacquerie, there were no major nationwide peasant uprisings. One could assume that neither rebellious peasants nor city dwellers nor nobles still challenged the absolute power of the king. This or that group might entertain dreams of changing the dynasty, increasing the power of the nobles, or receiving more privileges from the crown, but no one group seriously challenged the monarchy as an institution. This does not mean that the monarchy did not face serious challenges. These challenges were created by crimes that pestered authorities and society on a daily basis, and the state deployed its most repressive force against them. Criminals or "social" criminals—those whose social protest was interwoven with criminal activities—were a major permanent threat, and these problems were emphasized in contemporary historical chronicles.[37]

As in previous centuries, various forms of violence, often leading to murder, proliferated. The state tried to eliminate these crimes with the most decisive severity. In the fourteenth and first half of the fifteenth century, armed bands, often led by nobles and displaced mercenaries, posed a major threat to society. These required the focus of the state's repressive role. While the army continued as the potential source of banditry in the second half of the fifteenth century and into the sixteenth, its importance in spreading violent crime was reduced somewhat. This was due to the increasing discipline of the troops and the slow introduction of quasi-permanent detachments that were not dismissed after being discharged. The emerging rudimentary rural police and other measures taken by the authorities also reduced the threat from soldiers and their leaders. This made it possible for the state to focus its attention on ordinary criminals and more effectively use its resources in dealing with crime. The state ruthlessly dealt with the criminals, making little distinction between commoners and the elite.

Punishment of Murderers and Other Violent Offenders

Premeditated murder committed by anyone, including nobles, was punishable by death.[38] As discussed above, nobles were usually beheaded, for this was regarded as honorable. It was less painful than any other type of execution, if the executioner was qualified and sturdy and could chop off the head without much pain for the victim. Yet if he committed a type of crime regarded as "ignoble," even a noble could be hanged or undergo other types of torture and humiliating death.[39]

A noble could be hanged even if he committed a crime that was not regarded as dishonoring, such as murder. This happened with nobles who committed murder or other violent crimes after so-called "asseurement." "The asseurement was legally imposed prohibition of violence between two disputants, given at the request of one of the parties, binding for both of them and their kindred, of indefinite duration, the breach of which was a capital offense."[40] Breaking this rule was a very serious offense, and those who were guilty suffered the most degrading punishment. The social position of the culprit in such a case was not of much importance. "All juridical texts agreed that the penalty for any breach of asseurement was death by hanging."[41] Sometimes the culprit could be forgiven when the "victim suffered no worse than some bleeding." Those who committed murder or inflicted serious bodily harm were hanged regardless of social position. "There is no remission recorded for a breach resulting in mutilation, permanent physical damage, or death."

Even considerable numbers of culprits from the nobility were not decapitated. For this reason, one should concur with Foucault, who stated: "Decapitation was the most rare of executionary methods. It was reserved for nobles done with a heavy sword."[42] In many cases, death was the result of prolonged torture. Torture constituted the nature of the punishment and "executioners exercised 'every cruelty with regard to the evil-doing patients, treating them, buffeting and killing them as if they had a beast in their hands.'"[43]

There were numerous ways of dispatching the murderer in torturous ways. A person engaged in multiple murders could be quartered and both head and body parts were exposed to terrify potential culprits.[44] In this sort of death the brutality was visible, even more graphic and extreme. This was clear in procedures during which human bodies were actually dismembered in the same way animals are butchered. This sort of execution was macabre theater, and it was expected that common folk would attend these presentations in the same way that they were attracted to theatrical displays at market or at church. "The condemned man was blindfolded and tied to a stake; all around, on the scaffold, were stakes with iron hooks. The confessor whispered in the patient's ear and, after he had given him the blessing, the executioner, who had an iron bludgeon of the kind used in the slaughterhouses, delivered a blow with all his might on the temple of the wretch, who fell dead: The mortis exacter, who had a large knife, then cut his throat, which spattered him with blood."[45]

The brutal nature of the act, the sheer display of cruelty, was shocking even for those who witnessed it multiple times. One witness could hardly stand the spectacle and confessed to readers "it was a horrible sight to see." Yet the actual execution was only the beginning of the procedure: "The executioner continued with the ritual of dismembering the body: He severed the sinews near the two heels, and opened up the belly from which he drew the heart, liver, spleen and lungs, which he stuck on iron hooks, and cut and dissected into pieces, which he then stuck on the other hooks as he cut them, as one does with an animal." One could hardly observe such a horror, and the contemporaries who presented this scene to their readers added with a gloomy philosophic air: "Look who can at such a sight."

In the most important crimes, execution was even more elaborate, designed not just to prolong suffering but also to instruct spectators on the horrors of crime and punishment. One method involved mutilation, limited to crimes such as parricide; the parricide could also be burned at the stake.[46] The culprits had their arms cut off before the actual execution.[47] This could also be a punishment for those whose acts of arson led to the death of people.[48]

Banditry was punished with the same severity. The authorities assumed that bandits, or even those who were merely suspected of being bandits, should be treated without pity and be dispatched without further ado. In sixteenth-century Rouen, "of ten brigandage suspects who came before the Parlement only one escaped execution; he was a priest, whom the Parlement handed to the ecclesiastical courts for judgment. This severity is the more impressive in that these cases involved no actual taking of life."[49] The courts were equally cruel in dealing with those who broke from military discipline who could potentially be engaged in banditry.[50]

The state's repressive machinery did not discriminate against anyone in its terrorist practices, and women who engaged in murder were punished in the same way as men. They could be hanged for their crime.[51] Even if no deaths resulted from crimes, perpetrators could be punished with death for attempts on the life and property of individuals. For example, arson was punishable by hanging[52] or burning at the stake. Those who merely provoked arson could be banished.

This sort of punishment was recorded from an early date. According to one source, banishment began starting in the twelfth and thirteenth centuries and was employed "quite energetically" in the Middle Ages (183, 184, 223).[53] "The banishment from the locality implied 'expulsion without resources.'" This was a particularly miserable punishment. Those who were banished for fixed periods of time could preserve their property, but those expelled permanently lost their possessions, and this could lead to starvation (224-25). Those who returned to the locality without permission could be hanged (186). In the fourteenth century there were cases of punishment by incarceration and one could languish in prison for a long time (251-52). Conditions in the jail were appalling, and a slow and painful death could be the result.[54] Still, at the end of the Middle Ages/beginning of the modern era prisons were not a popular type of punishment.[55] They were mostly places of detainment before the actual punishment.

Crimes other than murder were also severely punished. In some cases fines could be used as punishment, even in cases of armed assault that did not result in death.[56] The authorities also tried to eliminate conditions that made violence possible and, by the fifteenth through sixteenth century, there was a movement for the disarmament of the population.[57] This also went along with the authorities' drive against dueling.[58] Those who engaged in this sort of crime could be punished by death, albeit this punishment was comparatively rare.[59] The royal restrictions on hunting were also designed to discourage expertise in the use of deadly weapons.[60]

Punishment for "Crimes against Nature"

The authorities were especially tough with murderers whose violations constituted what was usually called a crime "against nature." This term denoted crimes that seemed to be against human nature, for example, children killing their parents. These crimes were regarded as outrageous, for they offended the supposedly divine order, and for this reason some cultures denied the existence of such crimes.[61] This sort of crime was always punished with exceptional severity. The state also started to consider infanticide as such a crime and by the beginning of the modern era there appeared a policy intended to prevent parents from killing their children.

Infanticide as a crime is a modern notion. Medieval judicial practice was rather lenient in this regard, following the ancient practice that considered children the property of the parents. In ancient societies, children were often the only available form of "investment" and insurance. Support of parents was a paramount virtue in all ancient/traditional societies.[62] Boca reported that ancient tradition assumed parents had absolute power over their children and could dispose of their lives at will (180). Infanticide was directly related to the similar practice in the animal world where weak offspring are killed to reduce the demand for food when it is scarce. The weakling must be killed, for its survival endangered the existence of the community. This was the rationale for the Spartan practice of throwing weak newborns from a rock. In many peasant families, killing babies was a form of saving food, and thus a crude form of birth control. In medieval France killing babies could even have occult implications.[63] The idea that the parents, especially the head of the family, had strong power over the other members of the family, especially the children, was reinforced by the state as a way of disciplining society.[64]

By the dawn of the modern era, however, the state challenged the practice of infanticide. It had become a crime at least by the fifteenth century (180), and by the sixteenth it was definitely seen as a heinous crime "against nature." Mothers who killed their children could be executed, and a 1556 ordinance of Henri II (1556) stipulated that infanticide carried a mandatory death sentence.[65] Prosecution was justified on judicial and religious grounds. It was stated that the life of the baby was given by God and must not be taken arbitrarily. Moreover, the souls of babies murdered before official registration and baptism were deprived of the postmortem benefits of the true Christian.[66] The law not only protected children from being killed outright or abandoned, but also discouraged illegitimate births by preventing women from shifting responsibility for these children onto society. At the same time, the state encouraged legal adoption of these children.[67]

While mistreatment of a child that led to death was a crime, the law took into account the intent. If the woman had abandoned the child with the intention of saving him or her, she had a fair chance to escape the death sentence. The story was different when a child was abandoned with the clear intention to kill him or her or when infanticide was actually committed.[68] Another interpretation implied, however, that the intention of the mother was of no importance and "Despite the lack of direct evidence, the punishment for infanticide was most severe."[69] At least this was the interpretation of the 1556 law in sixteenth-century Rouen. "Concealment of pregnancy and failure to bring the child to be baptized were to be taken as indications that the mother had not wished for a child and had killed it. Despite the lack of direct evidence, the punishment of infanticide was always severe. Of twenty-two defendants, only two were not executed."[70]

While the mother and father were indeed responsible for the child's life, appropriate baptism, and nourishment, any guardian and in some cases the employer of the woman could also be found liable. This was, for example, the case with a domestic servant. "Legally, any child of a female servant conceived while she was in her employer's household was automatically considered the offspring of the master unless he could prove otherwise."[71] This rule not only emphasized the power of the head of household over the domestics, children included, but also underlined his responsibility for the child. While male members of society were implicitly responsible for child survival, mothers bore the main responsibility and were punished for lapses with exceptional severity.

Often women who killed their children were burned at the stake, as were those guilty of homosexuality, bestiality, and incest. The fire had a semi-religious implication for it purified both society and implicitly the guilty party.[72] "Burning was at an eight foot stake, around which kindling and wood were piled in a pyramid, with a hollow space near the stake and a passage for the executioner; only the victim's head protruded from the pile."[73] Infanticide could also lead to the punishment of being drawn.[74] There were various other ways in which mothers who killed or facilitated the death of their own children could be punished.

The number of mothers caught in bringing death to their children was initially small, as was the number of death sentences for this crime. Yet these numbers tended to increase steadily over the sixteenth and seventeenth centuries. In Paris, from 1539 to 1542, executions for infanticide were only 4 percent of the total number of executions, increasing to 15 percent by 1572, 18 percent by 1610, 32 percent by 1668-1670, and 34 percent by 1696-1698. When the authorities condemned these women to death, it specified the most degrading punishment. From 1539 to 1542, 60 percent of women condemned to death by the Parlement of Paris were hanged, increasing to 69 percent in 1572 and 89 percent by 1610.[75]

The state not only protected children from murder by their parents, but also tried to protect their property interests. There was also a provision from 1560 on to protect the property of children when their mothers remarried after the deaths of their fathers.[76]

To sum up, it was clear that the authorities relentlessly drove against any kind of violence, especially that which led to homicide. The death penalty in all its forms was largely reserved for these cases until the end of the ancien régime: "68% of death sentences were reserved for those who wantonly killed, maimed, or robbed."[77] This information is given for the eighteenth century, but one could assume that these numbers were characteristic of previous periods as well. The same was true of robbery. Robbery involving weapons concerned authorities the most. At the same time, the state, especially by the end of the ancien régime, was more lenient toward those who had not committed violence. "Only 31% of death sentences were for thefts or larceny without violence.... half of those were burglaries by breaking and entering, an implicitly violent and life-endangering crime." Indeed when the state demonstrated lenience, it was not toward hardened criminals with a penchant for violence. "Three-fourths of pardons were for those convicted of intentional (but not pre-meditative) murder, homicide, and injurious violence (usually in the course of brawls)." As above, the eighteenth-century numbers can reasonably be used to characterize the previous period.

Protection of Property

European states in general and the French absolutist state in particular focused their major efforts on the elimination of violent crime, and applied death sentences, in most cases employing torture and degrading death to punish the culprits. Some pundits (e.g., Foucault) explained this preoccupation of the state with eliminating people engaged in violence by citing the ideology prevailing at the end of the Middle Ages/early modern era. People were concerned with interpersonal relationships, and crime was seen as directed against persons rather than against property (contrary to the modern capitalist view, where private property is the sacred cornerstone of bourgeois civilization). This explanation hardly works. If it were true, the modern West with its developed capitalism would employ capital punishment for simple theft rather than for homicide. While different cultures and societies have different levels of tolerance of violence, no society tolerates private murder on a large scale or banditry. For example, Ottoman sultans negotiated with bandits not so much because of political culture, but because they lacked the strength to deal with bandits/rebels toughly. While all states reserve the toughest punishment for those who engage in violence, especially on a large scale, for example banditry or uprisings, all states also punish property offenders.

The desire to protect property did not necessarily depend on the importance of private property in the socioeconomic life of the society. In fact, the idea of private property could be negated completely, at least in regard to "means of production," yet heavy penalties be imposed on those who damaged or stole from the state or from private individuals. In Stalinist USSR, private property was quite limited. In fact, it was emphasized that the importance of the institution of private property was a cardinal characteristic of the bourgeois state. Yet one could be sent to the Gulag for a long time (with little chance to come back) for petty theft of state property. Those who stole from individual citizens could also be severely punished. The same could be said about the early modern state, France in particular. The idea of private property was underdeveloped, but the state took protection of property quite seriously and in most cases punished violations by death.

Tough punishment for murderers benefited the entire society, even if leaders of popular revolts were executed for murder and insurrection. Banditry and similar violent crimes were a danger to the populace as well as to the elite. The same could be said for protection of property. It is tempting to present protection of property as class bias on the part of the state, serving the interest of the elite. This interpretation was popular among historians on the Left in 1960-1970, who often saw any form of stealing as social defiance against the capitalist order. This view of the state approach to protection of property could be questioned, at least in medieval/early modern France. The object of thievery was the property of the rich, but of the poor as well. The peasantry, who constituted the vast majority of the population, hated thieves regardless of the fact that stealing was often limited to food or household items. This, of course, did not prevent them from stealing when the opportunity existed. Thus, as with violent crimes, the state both confronted the entire society and at the same time benefited the entire society in its terrorist activities.

Royal authorities regarded theft as a crime "most serious for the social order."[78] This explained "why theft, like murder, was liable to capital punishment"; in Paris from 1389 to 1392 prosecution of those engaged in thievery constituted 66.9 percent of all trials.[79] And the accused were treated harshly. "In Paris at the end of XIV century 87% of those who were condemned for theft by the judges in Chatelet were given capital punishment," usually hanged.[80]

Hanging seems to have been the most popular method of execution. According to some calculations, it was inflicted on 70 percent of those condemned to death in fifteenth-century Paris and in some provincial cities such as Avignon.[81] Hanging was regarded as not only painful but highly dishonorable.[82] In some cases, thieves were mutilated; parts of their bodies, presumably hands, were amputated.[83] Thievery was seen as a degrading crime, and even nobles who engaged in it, especially in the case of recidivism, could be hanged, a degrading and thus suitable punishment.[84]

It would wrong to assume that the state only protected the property of the elite. Those who stole animals crucial to the peasant household, such as horses, could also be condemned to death.[85] The usual punishment for horse thieves was hanging.[86] France was not an exception in dealing cruelly with theft. "English law was notorious for prescribing the death penalty for a vast range of offenses as slight as the theft of goods valued at twelve pence."[87]

In some cases the life of the thief could be spared. This was usually the case if the worth of stolen merchandise was rather small and if it was the first offense. Yet, even in these cases the punishment was severe. "A first theft might entail cutting off an ear or putting out an eye; at the second a foot or nose would be cut off; there was no excuse for a third theft—the thief was hanged."[88] In some cases the law required even tougher punishment. "A thief who repeated his offence three times should be punished in the same way as the man or woman who sheltered him; both were to be burned alive."[89] There were recorded cases where young women engaged in numerous thefts were buried alive. Gender did not save the culprit from the brutal punishment, nor was age in most cases any guarantee of leniency. In dealing with children the ancien régime demonstrated the severity of its legal system, fully shaped by the seventeenth century.

The assumption that repression is the only foundation of social stability could be seen in the ancien régime's approach to children. The legal culture of ancien régime France recognized differences between children and adults; "prepubescent children were not executed, banished, or sent to the galley, but minors did not enjoy immunity from penal liability."[90] A boy younger than twelve could be whipped in the court, and the youngster's parents were admonished to "be more attentive to his conduct." The youth could also be imprisoned, and those eighteen and older were punished as adults and the punishment could be quite cruel, even when the crime was comparably minor and committed because of fear of actual starvation.

The judicial machinery of the ancien régime also had little restraint in dealing with adults who were different from the majority. Indeed, if the unfortunate thief was a member of a religious minority, he or she could expect an even more painful and humiliating death than a Christian. Jews guilty of stealing, for example, could be hanged "by the feet" and "at each side of him a large dog would be hanged."[91] One Jew, informed of the nature of his future execution, expressed the immediate desire to be converted to Christianity. This wish was fulfilled, with the guards, warder, and warder's wife as godparents. After the ceremony of baptism, the culprit was duly hanged. While belonging to a religious minority, such as Judaism, usually was seen as an aggravating condition, the same could be said in regard to those who were perceived as belonging to marginal groups, such as vagabonds. "In Paris it was sufficient for any accused criminal to be labeled as one in order to ensure his execution regardless of his actual misdeeds."[92]

Those who encroached upon the property of the king or endangered the interests of the state in some other way could not expect leniency.

They usually ended their lives in the most horrible way. Those who forged money could be drawn in boiling water, and their property confiscated.[93] It might be added that death by drawing was regarded as particularly dishonorable. It seems that in some cases forgers, apparently especially women, were hanged.[94] Execution also awaited those who encroached directly on the property of the crown, such as wild game, historically seen as the property of the king and the nobles who had exclusive rights for hunting. Therefore, those who engaged in poaching could be condemned to death from the time of Louis XI.[95]

Punishment for Sexual Transgression

No society can exist with violence and unauthorized assaults on the lives of the people. No society can allow theft of property by individuals. This is the case even with states that discard the notion of private property completely, such as the Stalinist USSR. In every state, coercion, if needed, violent coercion has been employed to maintain basic order, even if this meant the transformation of the state along totalitarian lines. This was the case with the French state in the fourteenth through sixteenth centuries, when violence and attacks on property required coercion and an extreme form of state-sponsored terror against violence and attacks on property.

The same could be said about sexual culture. The model of sexual behavior has also been different in different cultures, but regardless of the cultural and historical framework, no society can exist without some regulation of the sexual relationship. There are rules for sexual interaction in all societies. In many cultures male coercion was seen as an essential sign of virility and passion. Yet there was a limit on the level of coercion men could impose on women. Society also tried to "normalize" violent sexual behavior by legalizing it in the context of custom and tradition as with the widespread tradition of kidnapping the bride. But no society could legalize rape in its most brutal form—sexual intercourse against the woman's will which led to severe injury or death and where momentary gratification was the motive.

There was also variety in the forms of families, along with structural similarities. Every society had a tendency to stabilize the family and to prevent activities, for example, seduction, that could lead to disruption. Even cultures that had benevolent attitudes toward sexual appetites tried to institutionalize practices and construct a family of a sort. This was, for example, the case with harems. No society approved of "free love" (relationships outside any judicial or traditional framework) as the cornerstone of the sexual relationship.

In early modern Europe the breakdown of the sexual relationship was part of the general social and political meltdown, and there was a tendency for the state to respond with severity. In France in the fourteenth through sixteenth centuries the state engaged in rigorous enforcement of the sexual order. It employed various types of repression, from the death penalty and castration to expulsion to "puritanizing" the sexual life of society, taking this term holistically. The severity of the state's response was due to the fact that sexual misdeeds not only contributed to crime, but also played a considerable role in spreading pandemic diseases such as syphilis.

While the intellectual/cultural aspects of the spread of capitalism played a role in this "puritanization," it was actually not related to capitalism or any other political ot cultural environment. As in repressing violence and violation of property, every state followed to some degree the same road. The broad sexual-social meltdown led the state to follow a totalitarian line, regardless of ideological or social frameworks. Stalinist USSR attempted the "puritanization" of sexual mores in a way that seemed surprisingly similar to the process in early modern Europe. The attempt to regulate the sexual life of subjects of the French state had visible features of the Orwellian society of the watchful and controlling "Big Brother."

This drive against sexual immorality and the restriction of sexual life was fully integrated into the general drive for more order and control by the end of the sixteenth century. "From the sixteenth to the seventeenth century, France witnessed a gradual transition from one system of order to another, the latter exhibiting profoundly authoritarian characteristics. Discipline was a byword of the renewed morality of order, and fundamentally, the passions. By association, women were deemed most in need of discipline."[96] While one might see in this drive for sexual discipline a sort of anti-woman bias, it was actually much broader, directed against all sexes and social groups. Even the king was not absolutely free from the increasing drive for sexual probity. For example, "charges of effeminacy and gross sexual misconduct" were used to discredit Henri III.[97] His homosexuality was connected to violation of the natural religious order and to an assortment of other crimes including tyranny.[98]

According to this line of thinking, both religious and sexual crimes violated the divine order; this sameness was manifested by the fact that people who engaged in sexual crimes (e.g., sodomy) and in religious crimes (e.g., heresy) were often punished in the same way, by being burned at the stake.[99] "Judges were particularly receptive" to the sexual-family related crimes that in their view violated the foundation of the divine order.[100]

Punishment for Rape

Medieval law saw rape as an offense punishable by death; indeed, beginning in the thirteenth century, rapists who used direct force were punished by hanging.[101] Yet in d'Abbeville the person was apparently usually subject to lighter punishment such as banishment.[102] This often benign approach to rape had the same roots as disregard of theft, especially petty theft, and their concern with punishment of those engaged in serious physical violence.

Society's concern with physical violence in some ways explained the rather ambivalent approach to rape. According to Jeffrey Richards, medieval church law did not condemn rape.[103] It was, of course, inconceivable that any society regarded rape as a normal method of satisfying sexual appetite. Even if one assumes that the culture of sexual machismo implied violence as an element of erotic activity or an excusable manifestation of passion, one cannot believe that society would allow unrestricted force against women. The chronicles constantly emphasize that rape was among the horrible evils of war. The rather soft approach to punishment for sexual violence could be explained in different ways. With all the trauma of rape, women were still more concerned with not having their throats cut or being seriously maimed. Since these violent occurrences were quite common, they became the major concern of the authorities with their limited resources. However, the state never ignored rape or other sexually related crimes. Even in the Middle Ages, there were recorded cases of brutal punishment for them. As the state increased its vigor in prosecuting all types of crime, prosecution for rape became more widespread and severe.

The punishment for rape increased by the beginning of the modern era, and by the fourteenth and fifteenth centuries it was punishable by death.[104] The adulterer and the rapist could suffer a shameful and painful punishment such as public castration.[105] Castration as a form of punishment was employed at least from the thirteenth century onward. In contemporary pictures, one can see how the procedure was carried out. A guard with unsheathed sword pulled the undergarment of the malefactor over his head while the executioner cut off the testicles. Two other guards, fully armed, stood in the presence of the execution.[106]

Due to the proliferation of violent and especially group rape, it seems that prevention of this sort of crime was a major goal of the authorities, and perpetrators were punished with vigor as time progressed. The authorities were also quite concerned with the rape of virgins. The emotional aspect of the crime was not of the greatest concern. Rather, there was an overriding notion that loss of virginity outside marriage tainted the woman. It dramatically reduced her chance for a good marriage, in many cases any marriage, and ruined her economic, social, and emotional life. For these reasons the court operated on the principle that *virginitas corrupta est enormis crimen* (corruption of the virgin is an enormous crime).[107] When indicting dangerous criminals, the authorities emphasized that the criminal was not merely a murderer and rapist but the rapist of a virgin. The rape of virgins aggravated his crime considerably.[108]

An even graver offense was the rape of female children. The sense of the heinousness of this crime was shared not only by the authorities and public, but also by some habitual rapists, who in most cases raped only women of marriageable age. One reason for their avoidance of raping children was that the punishment for this crime was "expedient and rigorous."[109]

A male could engage in illicit extramarital sex and destroy a female's reputation not just through direct violence, but also through deception (false promises of marriage), and even seductive flattery. In these cases he could be prosecuted for using compliments and flattery to gain sexual access, seen as "moral rape."[110] Even if the seducer was not able to achieve his goal, solicitation could damage the woman's reputation. There was a popular assumption that persistence of the solicitor was due not to the woman's wealth or even beauty, but mostly to her frivolous behavior. For this reason "asseurement" was used when women wanted "means to rid themselves of importunate would-be seducers."[111] The man would swear before a magistrate not to harass the woman in the future. If he persisted afterward, he could be severely punished.

A person did not need to be a dangerous sexual predator or grossly violate prescribed norms of sexual behavior to undergo castration. In Avignon, under the rule of popes, this could be the punishment of a Jew who engaged in sexual relations with a Christian.[112] Jews were seen here not as a racial but as a religious group. Castration was just one of numerous tortures if the sexual crime had political implications. This was the case with the Aulnay brothers, who engaged in affairs with Philippe IV's daughter-in-law. The sexual encounters could be seen as high treason. It was not surprising that the culprits experienced various tortures "cum genitalibus amputatis."[113]

By the sixteenth century, punishment for fornication became less brutal. In most cases the guilty party, for example a married man involved

with an unmarried woman, was "heavily fined and given written warn-
ings not to associate with each other in a scandalous fashion."[114] While
the punishment for marital infidelity or sex with a married woman or
man ceased to be as brutal as before, it became more egalitarian. In the
fourteenth and fifteenth centuries, a man of high social position would
not be punished, at least as severely, if he engaged in sex with a woman
of low social status, especially if she was his domestic. Difference of
social position continued to play a role in determining punishment. But
the man's immunity was no longer guaranteed. There were recorded
cases when married men were punished for having sex with women
domestics.[115]

Even when there was no break of marriage or seduction of unaware
women, when two consenting adults lived together, the state still in-
tervened and usually ordered them to pay a fine. The man was usually
punished more severely than the woman, especially if there was a suspicion that he had deflowered the woman. If the man proclaimed that
he intended to marry the woman, and she agreed, it was regarded as a
mitigating circumstance. But there was still a fine because the man lived
with the woman without formal marriage. In some cases even assertions
about imminent marriage did not provide mitigating circumstances and
both men and women paid a heavy fine.[116]

There were other important aspects to monitoring and controlling
sexual relationships. In the past the state had not been much interested
in illicit affairs unless there were direct complaints or what "scandal,"
meaning inappropriate behavior that undermined the existing value
system. To be sure, scandalous behavior and complaints aggravated
guilt and attracted the attention of the officials. But absence of scandal
and complaint did not solve the problems. The state engaged in detailed
investigations of those suspected of unlawful sexual activity. Dining
together could be seen as a sign of an unlawful liaison.[117]

Control over Marriage

The authorities were also concerned with exactly what constituted
"rapt," a term implying the seduction of a girl, often done to force marriage. Marriage implied the transfer of property as the woman's dowry
or inheritance. This aspect of "rapt" was of the greatest concern to the
relatives of the woman and to the authorities. There were other sides of the
"rapt," an implication that sex was the final goal. These affairs were also
quite damaging for the woman, for they ruined her reputation, especially
if the seducer was a person of lower social status. In these cases, justice

looked at even consensual sexual relationships in the same way American law sees consensual relationships between minors and adults. This was "statutory rape." The difference lies in the fact that in the sixteenth century the woman was not considered able to control her passion until age twenty-five.[118] The crime was aggravated if the woman was entrusted to the man as her servant. One could view this situation as a combination of "sexual harassment" and "statutory rape." Even if the liaison led to marriage, it did not save the man from serious complications.

In June 1546, Henri II issued his "famous edict" of Avignon that invalidated marriages performed without consent of the parents.[119] As time progressed, the severity of punishment for "rapt" increased. According to the ordinance of Blois (1579), all "rapt" could lead to a death sentence in aggravating circumstances such as the young age of the seduced girl or low social position of the seducer.[120] This emphasis on death as punishment made the ordinance of Blois different from previous edicts that merely dissolved clandestine marriages.[121] The edict of 1579 promised violators a certain death sentence and made sure they could not expect royal pardon.[122] Even though in most cases the court did not condemn the guilty party to death, the penalty was serious. The marriage was annulled despite the fact that marriage in all other cases was seen as irrevocable.[123] The guilty party paid a heavy penalty, even if he avoided the death penalty.[124]

The authorities were mostly concerned with the man as potential seducer and evildoer. But the spirit of the law was much broader, and there were cases when the female was found guilty of "rapt," seducing and marrying without parental consent.[125] The notion of "rapt" severely limited young adults in their search for partners, either for sex or for marriage. In many respects it was the reversal of a centuries-old trend and the return of a time of patriarchal slavery when the father had absolute power over members of his household. This reversal could also be seen in the 1567 law, according to which "servants could not marry without their masters' permission."[126]

The state also tried to eradicate all other forms of illegal sexual liaisons. Bigamy was a gross violation of both civil and religious law, and bigamists were severely punished.[127] In the fourteenth century, there was already a drive against adultery and concubinage.[128] The Counter-Reformation also led to a drive against immoral clergy behavior, such as concubinage.[129]

By the sixteenth and seventeenth centuries, public castration and genital amputation were mostly gone. Yet the state had not reduced the severity of punishment for what it regarded as criminal sexual activity. Some activities were still punished in a most severe way. This was the case with crimes "against nature." One example was bestiality, of which there were several recorded cases in thirteenth-century d'Abbeville. There were also recorded cases of homosexuality. While the law stipulated the death sentence for the crime, a sodomite in d'Abbeville was usually banished.[130] Still, even in the Middle Ages, the treatment of those engaged in homosexuality and bestiality was not always lenient. There were recorded cases when those engaged in bestiality were burned at the stake,[131] and as time progressed, the state increased its repressiveness in this respect. Pedophiles and homosexuals could be burned at the stake or end their lives on the wheel.[132] Sodomy was considered directly related to heresy, as a violation of divine law, and punished in the same way.[133]

Control over Prostitution

Prostitution constitutes one of the best examples of social-sexual malfunction. As a form of antisocial sexuality, prostitution and prostitutes have been despised and hated in practically all cultures. Comparison of this or that activity to prostitution was always a synonym for the final moral degradation. Even males who patronized brothels and cavorted with streetwalkers were adamant that the label "prostitute" must never be attached to their wives, daughters, and relatives. In early modern Europe in general and France in particular, prostitution led not only to various asocial processes such as crime and disintegration of the family, but also to the proliferation of disease. Thus authorities tried to repress and regulate prostitution early on, even at a time when the phenomenon was still broadly tolerated. Regulation was seen as away to reduce the harmful effects of prostitution, with the side benefit of making the profession profitable for the treasury. Pressure and repression against prostitution increased by the sixteenth century.

The drive against asocial sexuality, for example, prostitution, did not always imply direct repression. Institutionalization and regulation could make asocial sexuality less harmful and in some cases even benefit society. This approach can be seen in some modern countries of the West, such as the Netherlands, where prostitution was institutionalized and integrated into the mainstream of society. This integration not only reduced the negative implications for the rest of society, but also created income (tax on prostitution) for the Dutch treasury. Regulation of prostitution and asocial sexuality in general was widespread in the Middle Ages/early modern era.

Prostitution was legitimized in some regions for practical reasons. The assumption was that it would provide an outlet for sexual desire and divert people from crimes such as gang rape.[134] Authorities saw gang rape not as the twisted entertainment of youngsters who engaged in it regardless of the nature of their sexual lives but as caused by an unsatisfied sex drive: young people unable to find sex turned to rape. In this context, gang rape was akin to the starving looting bread shops. Thus, political stability required government intervention. The brothel became "state property" and a quasi-socialist enterprise. While socializing the sex trade and regulating supply, or at least a considerable part of it, the city also set prices. The principle of free market capitalism in which prostitutes or managers of brothels established prices was discarded. Officials succeeded in regulating the price of sex—as affordable as bread. "The price of sexual intercourse in these public brothels was cheap, amounting to about one-eight or one-tenth of a journeyman's daily salary. So bachelors, forbidden to have sexual intercourse with so-called honest girls or women, nevertheless had sexual activities with so-called public or common girls."[135]

This vision of sex as an essential commodity to be provided either for a low price or free was not something special. Ancient Rome had a sort of charitable sex service, and the populace could find similar phenomena during the Bolshevik Revolution in Russia, with the "socialization of women." This approach to sex—as an essential yet harmful commodity—induced medieval French authorities to regulate the sex trade in the same fashion as the bread trade.

Regulation of sexual life started early. Attempts to control French prostitution had its origins in the thirteenth century, during the reign of Louis IX.[136] Supervising prostitution in Paris was entrusted to a special official, the "roi de ribauds" (king of ribaldry). The first official mention of this salaried position was in 1214. Later, similar officials emerged in other French cities, where they could be called "king of amorous life."[137]

There were increased attempts to control the activities of prostitutes in the cities by the fifteenth century.[138] Prostitution was controlled in d'Abbeville from that period. Observing their activities and controlling their behavior were entrusted to the local executioner, an additional responsibility to his major job of dispatching people.[139] There were also attempts to limit prostitution to well-defined districts of the city and times of day.[140] There were also attempts to differentiate prostitutes from other women; in some fifteenth-century French cities, prostitutes were required to wear a certain mark on their clothes.[141]

Access to prostitutes was institutionalized for both elite and populace. There was an organized sex service for distinguished city residents and their guests. Casual and diversified sex was seen as being as necessary as food and drink. The dignified members of society could not eat and drink the same food and beverages as the lower classes. Thus, efforts were made to institutionalize providing them diversified, high quality food and drink. Sex was also essential for male life, and males of high social status should have diverse sex in the same way as types of food and drink. At least in Paris, a special institution was created to provide sex services. "From 1214 to 1449 there was a King of Ribalds in the royal household in Paris, supervising the prostitutes resident there for use by the palace staff and guests."[142] While financial and social stability were the major reason for the toleration and even promotion of prostitution, there were other reasons as well. Philippe Augustus (1180-1223) "encouraged prostitution in Paris in order to discourage homosexuality among the students."[143]

There were also cases when the authorities tried to eliminate the evil of prostitution completely. There were recorded cases as early as the fourteenth century when women accused of debauched behavior, undoubtedly some of them prostitutes, were driven from French cities.[144] In 1420-1430 Arras, for example, there was an attempt to rid the town of prostitutes.[145] Some municipal brothels were closed even before the royal ordinance forbade them. In Toulouse "the municipal bordel was finally closed in 1557."[146] In Burgundy, prostitutes and pimps were beaten and imprisoned.[147] By the sixteenth century there was an increasing intolerance of prostitution.[148] Prostitution was increasingly repressed for various reasons. It was seen as being part of the criminal milieu. The rising respect for the family and marriage entailed increasing sacredness of religious legal obligations. All these had created problems for prostitution in earlier centuries, but by the sixteenth century, a new problem, syphilis, reinforced the old ones. Prostitution became related to the spread of venereal disease.[149] The desire to eliminate this threat was not much verbalized by the authorities, who dwelt more on moral and social implications of prostitution; it is quite likely that fear of venereal disease pushed society in general to deal with prostitution with such severity. It contributed mightily to the drive to puritanize sexual mores and increase control over societal behavior in general.[150]

However, despite all the limitations, prostitution remained legal until 1561, when, responding "to demands of the Third estate at the Estates General in Orleans," the crown "banned all brothels in [the] kingdom."[151]

The official prohibition to operate in Paris came later than in the other cities, possibly because the prostitutes there had an influential clientele. Nevertheless, this did not mean that prostitutes were free to engage in their trade in Paris in the first half of the sixteenth century. Regulations already specified the clothing they could wear and the regions of the city where they could operate. The 1565 edict outlawed brothels in Paris and stipulated that prostitutes and any debauched women be expelled "from Paris and suburbs in 24 hours."[152]

The drive against prostitution was primarily pragmatic—prostitution encouraged crime, disrupted families, and spread of venereal diseases. But the drive also had quasi-political and quasi-religious implications. Prostitution desecrated marriage. The union between France and the monarchy was seen as a sort of marriage, an interpretation made obvious in the coronation oath of Henri II, which included the statement that the king "took France as a bride."[153] Terrestrial marriage was also a spiritual marriage with the church.[154] Prostitution therefore desecrated the royal power, the entire social and divine order.

Repression and the Struggle against Disease

One of the major concerns of people in the early modern era was disease. Only famines could compete with disease for sheer destructiveness. Prevention of disease often involved state coercion, and various restraints were imposed on life and behavior in European countries. A variety of social and asocial processes led to the spread of disease, including increases in trade as well as migration of armies and vagabonds. The rapid growth of cities led to chaotic and dangerous building arrangements, which could lead to fire but, even more importantly, to an increase in garbage and human and animal refuse. These manifestations of bio-asociality, so to speak, encouraged the spread of pandemic disease.

The authorities tried in various ways to improve living conditions. As engineering arrangements were made, there were improvements in methods of dumping garbage and cleaning streets. Changes in morals and general improvement of sanitary conditions were an important method of preventing the spread of disease, but not the only way. The increase and repressiveness of police control was one of the most important elements. Foucault usually tried to attribute the rise of the police in the modern era to changes in the "episteme," which in his interpretation was unrelated to social conditions and actually shaped them. However, one is compelled to acknowledge that the rise of police surveillance in many cases was directly related to the spread of pandemic diseases. In these situations, the state and society started watching and controlling residents of the cities. Indeed the centralized power of the emerging absolutist state started to deal with these problems in the same way as with criminals, vagabonds, and the mentally ill (those who created problems for society as a whole, not just the state or elite).

Plague was a major problem in the late medieval/early modern era. Plague and famine (they often walked hand in hand) killed many more people than all wars. It is not surprising that the state implemented tough measures to stop the spread of disease. In this case the state was even more brutal than in its dealings with criminals. This brutal repression worked against people who often had not violated any societal rule and whose only "guilt" was that they were or could be infected with disease. At the same time, the authorities attempted to change people's social/behaviorist practices to improve sanitary conditions.

The Black Death in the fourteenth century caused the first serious attempts in this direction. There was an attempt to impose hygienic rules to fight plague as early as 1350, the worst plague years.[155] Authorities tried to increase the prestige of those who cleaned cesspools. A royal edict proclaimed that anyone who insulted these people would be fined.[156] In 1372 the authorities made the first edict against "the time-honored Parisian custom of throwing filth in the street by night."[157] "In 1370 *prevot* Hugues Aubriot built the first covered sewer at the rue Montmartre," and implicitly encouraged the people to use these facilities.[158] Severe punishment was implied for those who violated the rules. Until the beginning of the sixteenth century, Parisians placed chamber pots "in front of the door and workers passed by at assigned hours in the morning and afternoon to empty them.... Royal ordinances in the 1530s overturned this system by requiring the construction of cesspools." Fines were levied against "anyone who did not build a privy in his house or any citizens who were caught 'doing their necessities' publicly in the street" and salespersons who sold food of bad quality.[159]

The authorities also started to realize that not just feces and urine could create problems. By the sixteenth century the idea of a direct connection between the dirtiness of the street and plague had penetrated the minds of some of the medical profession in Paris, and they encouraged cleaning streets.[160] They also convinced authorities to move slaughterhouses outside the cities.[161] There were other attempts to improve the general sanitary conditions in the city, usually reinforced by doses of repression. In some sixteenth-century cities those who threw garbage on the street were imprisoned or publicly beaten.[162]

As in the previous century, while emphasizing the importance of restriction and punishment in preserving public health, the state was also engaged in the amelioration of living conditions, with positive implications for sanitation in the city. By the beginning of the sixteenth century, Paris had seventeen fountains[163] that played an important role in providing fresh water. And as one could assume, the punishment was severe for those who polluted or damaged the fountains. (While the supply of fresh water was important to fight epidemics, it had another important implication for the safety of the cities—the fight against fire.[164] The increase of the number of fountains definitely helped the authorities to deal with the problem.)

The attempt to restrain bio-asociality—to compel residents to take care of sanitary conditions—was not the only way authorities tried to eradicate disease. One of the earliest ways to control spread of disease was isolation of the infected. Leprosariums for the segregation of infected persons can be traced to the Persian Empire.[165] By the Middle Ages, this practice was widespread and required considerable correlation of activities on the part of authorities of all sorts, the church, and the public. "In the middle of the twelfth century, France had more than 2,000 leprosariums, and England and Scotland 220 for a population of a million and a half people."[166] Society imposed restrictions on the lives of lepers, sending them to the leprosarium if they violated the rules that segregated them from the rest of the population.[167] When the plague began to spread, the treatment was the same, isolating infected or potentially infected people, and in the sixteenth century expelling them from cities under the threat of death.[168] There was also an attempt to prevent the spread of contagious diseases from overseas. The first attempt at a system of quarantine was made at the end of the fifteenth century, and its development continued through the sixteenth century.[169]

In most cases both the pressure over the populace and the results were modest. But some outbreaks of plague in the fifteenth and sixteenth centuries led to quite radical measures of control that could easily be compared with the actions of the Nazi and Soviet regimes. Committees created to deal with the epidemic often received extraordinary power.[170] When in 1580 the plague struck Paris, the "neighboring towns created a blockade around the capital, refusing either to admit travelers and goods from the city or to deliver food and provisions for fear of contamination."[171] Authorities were apparently hardly concerned with the fact that lack of provisions could lead to starvation of some of the population, mostly the poor, who did not have enough stores of food.

In some cases the authorities tried to close public meeting places, where there was a chance of transmitting disease, public brothels in particular.[172] But these measures often did not work, and fear led to drastic measures as many thousands of people were sacrificed to save the rest. One drastic measure was to barricade people inside infested houses. These people would surely die, but it was assumed that these sacrifices would save the lives of others. One of the first examples of such measures could be seen in Milan in 1348. There were also expulsions of those who could be suspected in the spread of disease.[173] The fact that most of these people would die of disease and starvation did not bother the rest. Some neighborhoods were burned to prevent the spread of the plague; in Bordeaux an entire city quarter was burned in 1348. Similar measures were undertaken in the sixteenth century.[174]

As the epidemic continued in France, other drastic measures continued to be implemented with utmost severity. For example, in several outbreaks of the plague in late sixteenth-century Paris those suspected of being infested were forcibly evicted from their houses and sent to the crowded Hotel Dieu.[175] Their desperate resistance was justifiable, "the conditions of the hospitalizations were terrible," and deportation there was tantamount to a death sentence.[176] There were also recorded cases when those suspected of being infected were killed outright.[177]

Indeed, executions were seen as therapeutic measures. Prisoners infested with plague were killed.[178] Especially if they were burned (an act of purification), this extermination implied the eradication of both the disease and the "social disease": criminals. This practice would be repeated at the time of the French Revolution, during the September days when the crowd lynched not only aristocrats—the political criminals—but also "diseased whores," the source of biological and social pollution. This explains why in some cases brothels were closed and prostitutes were chased out of cities at the time of the plague, as in fifteenth-century Toulouse.[179] Terror fell not only on the infested, but also on those who took advantage of the confusion. The epidemic often led to confusion, which facilitated pillage. The response to this problem was draconian. Pillage along with acts of aggression during the plague could lead to the death sentence.[180]

While pandemic disease could affect anyone, some groups were more susceptible and more likely transmitters of disease. Society started to deal with marginal groups like vagabonds and beggars in harsh ways. Vagabonds were also suspected of being the cause of disease, the people who transmitted it. Thus, expulsion and incarceration of vagabonds was due to more than fear of crime and desire to use them for work details. The implications were both social and medical. Isolating these people from society so they could not spread disease and crime had both physical and mental implications. As time progressed, isolation and regulation embraced an increasing number of these people.

Thus, in its wide application of terror, the state struck not just at what could be seen as social opposition, whether rebellious peasants or nobles, but against a variety of asocial processes ranging from murder to emptying chamber pots in the street. Terror was a major tool in disciplining society. In this struggle against asocial processes, the state was often almost alone and had no other legitimacy or support but itself.

The dialectic of the struggle for order implied not only the totality of confrontation but also the totality of support. While the state might confront the entire population, it could rely on the support of the same population. Despite their asocial drives, all segments of the population were aware that they needed the king's absolute power above them, to protect society from itself. The early modern state was weak and therefore widely employed terror in facing the continuous social and asocial threats from all segments of society. Slowly, the state started to develop the apparatus of repression and control that would provide more stability and security in the future.

Notes

1. Claude Fouret, "Douai au XVIe siècle: une sociabilité de l'agression," *Revue d'Histoire Moderne et Contemporaine* 34 (January-March 1987): 23.
2. Geremek, *The Margins*, 13.
3. Simmel, *On Individuality*, 167.
4. Potter, "Rigueur de justice," 265.
5. Dewald, "The 'Perfect Magistrate,'" 295.
6. Ibid., 296.
7. Gonthier, *Le châtiment du crime*, 92, 93.
8. Chiffoleau, *Les justices*, 242.
9. Geremek, *The Margins*, 16.
10. Cuttler, *The Law*, 241, 242.
11. Bernard Schnapper, "Les peines arbitraires du XIIIe au XVIIIe siècle (doctrines savantes et usages français)," *Revue d'Histoire du Droit/ Legal History Review* 42, 1 (1974): 91-92.
12. John H. Langbein, *Torture and the Law of Proof: Europe and England in the Ancien Régime* (Chicago: University of Chicago Press, 1977), 11.
13. Schnapper, "Les peines arbitraires," 110.
14. Langbein, *Torture*, 55.
15. Cuttler, *The Law*, 154.
16. Schnapper, "Les peines arbitraires," 71.
17. Garnot, "La legislation et la repression des crimes," 86.
18. Schnapper, "Les peines arbitraires," 96; Potter, "Rigueur de justice," 267.

19.   Bernard Schnapper, "La repression du vagabondage et sa signification historique du XIVe au XVIIIe siècle," *Revue Historique de Droit Français et Étranger* 63 (1985): 149.
20.   Nicole Gonthier, "Prisons et prisonniers à Lyon aux XIVe et Xve siècles," *Mémoires de la Société pour l'Histoire du Droit et des Institutions des Anciens Pays Bourguignons, Comtois et Romands* 39 (1982): 27.
21.   Langbein, *Torture*, 3.
22.   Hanawalt and Wallace, "Introduction," xii.
23.   Gonthier, *Délinquance*, 210.
24.   Cuttler, *The Law*, 91.
25.   Dewald, "The 'Perfect Magistrate'," 295.
26.   Bernard Schnapper, "La justice criminelle rendue par le parlement de Paris sous le regne de François 1er," *Revue Historique de Droit Français et Etranger* 52, 2 (1974): 262.
27.   Langbein, *Torture*, 46.
28.   According to Herodotus, the Persians were rather conservative, assuming that men could receive pleasure only by making love to females. As they became more cosmopolitan; they "learn and then acquire the habit of all kinds of divertissements from various parts of the word, including the practice of having sex with boys, which they learnt from the Greeks." *The Histories*, 62.
29.   Langbein, *Torture*, 46.
30.   Gonthier, *Délinquance*, 249. The wheel, institutionalized in the sixteenth century, was known at least from the fourteenth.
31.   Foucault, *Discipline and Punish*, 32.
32.   Lebigre, "Quand la torture osait dire son nom," 6.
33.   Foucault, *Discipline and Punish*, 32.
34.   Ibid., 12.
35.   Norbert Elias, *The History of Manners: The Civilizing Process* (New York: Pantheon, 1982), 1: 204.
36.   Braudel, *The Identity*, 2: 385.
37.   Early modern France could be compared to Stalinist USSR. According to some historians, the Great Purges of the 1930s affected mostly common criminals whose crimes were "politicized" by authorities so they became enemies of the Soviet regime. Vadim Volkov, "The Concept of Kul'turnost': Notes on the Stalinist Civilizing Process," in *Stalinism: New Directions*, ed. Sheila Fitzpatrick (London: Routledge, 1999), 215. One might challenge but not completely disregard the assumption of purely political/social repression in Stalinist Russia. The turmoil released huge amounts of anomie, with which the state dealt harshly. Stalinist repression was directed not only at opposition to the regime (real or imaginary), but also against common, low criminals. Paul M. Hagenloh, "'Social Harmful Enemies' and the Great Terror," in *Stalinism*, 288-95.
38.   Authorities were usually more lenient toward unpremeditated types of murder. Esther Cohen, "Violence Control in Late Medieval France," *Legal History Review* 51 (1983): 121.
39.   Benoit Garnot, *Crime et justice aux XVIIe et XVIIIe siècles* (Paris: Imago, 2000), 125.
40.   Cohen, "Violence Control," 112.
41.   Ibid., 116.
42.   Richard Andrews, *Law, Magistracy, and Crime in Old Regime Paris, 1735-1789* (Cambridge: Cambridge University Press, 1990), 78.
43.   Foucault, *Discipline and Punish*, 51.

44. Schnapper, "Justice criminelle," 269.
45. Foucault, *Discipline and Punish*, 51.
46. Schnapper, "Justice criminelle," 266, 269.
47. Garnot, *Crime et justice*, 127.
48. Alfred Soman, "Sorcellerie, justice criminelle et société dans la France moderne: l'égo-histoire d'un américain a Paris," *Histoire, Economie et Société* 12, 2 (1993): 199.
49. Dewald, "The 'Perfect Magistrate,'" 296. On the increasing harshness of punishment during the sixteenth century, see also Leah Otis, "Nisi in Postribulo: Prostitution in Languedoc from the Twelfth to the Sixteenth Century" (Ph.D. dissertation, Columbia University, 1980), 99.
50. Pictures of the era represent mass executions with soldiers hanging like fruit from tree branches.
51. Gonthier, *Le châtiment du crime*, 148.
52. Boca, *La justice*, 209, 207 (citations in text in parentheses); Delumeau and Lequin, *Les malheurs*, 267.
53. See also Geremek, *The Margins*, 19-20.
54. Chiffoleau, *Les justices*, 227; Geremek, *The Margins*, 18.
55. Geremek, *The Margins*, 17.
56. Fouret, "Douai," 7.
57. Gonthier, *Le châtiment du crime*, 55.
58. François Billaçois, *Le duel dans la société française des Xve-XVIIe siècles: essai de psychosociologie historique* (Paris: Ecole des Hautes Etudes en Sciences Sociales, 1986), 92, 146-47.
59. In 1599 the Paris Parlement interdicted the duel as a "crime de lèse-majesté."Duels were also interdicted by the church at the 1563 Council of Trent. François Billaçois, "La grande époque du duel," *Histoire* 87 (1986): 31. See also Jorge Arditi, *A Genealogy of Manners: Transformations of Social Relations in France and England from the Fourteenth to the Eighteenth Century* (Chicago: University of Chicago Press, 1998), 131. On dueling, see also Andrews, *Law*, 77.
60. Arditi, *A Genealogy*, 78.
61. Ancient Persia could be an example. A child who killed his parents was asserted to be not a natural child, but an adopted child born to other parents. Herodotus, *The Histories*, 63.
62. Some cultures were exceptions, according to Herodotus. For example, a son could choose not to support his father if he was irresponsible. However, a daughter was required to support her father regardless of her treatment. *The Histories*, 619.
63. Garnot, "La legislation et la repression," 80.
64. In some cases strengthening the power of the head of the family limited the wife's property rights, as did 1510 customary law. Carol L. Loats, "Gender and Work in Sixteenth-Century Paris" (Ph.D. dissertation, University of Colorado, 1993), 132. Here the state appealed to Roman law. Mark Cummings, "Elopement: Family, and the Courts: The Crime of Rape in Early Modern France," *Proceedings of the Annual Meeting of the Western Society for French History* 4 (1976): 120.
65. Schnapper, "Justice criminelle," 272; Schnapper, "Les peines arbitraires," 98; Philip F. Riley "Women and Police in Louis XIV's Paris," *Eighteenth Century Life* 9, 2 (1977): 39.
66. Garnot, "La legislation et la repression," 80.
67. Kristin Elizabeth Gager, "'Comme leur propre enfant': Adoption of Children and Domestic Boundaries in Sixteenth- and Seventeenth-Century Paris" (Ph.D. dissertation, Princeton University, 1992), 146, 245.

68. James R. Farr, *Authority and Sexuality in Early Modern Burgundy (1550-1730)* (New York: Oxford University Press, 1995), 131.
69. Dewald, "The 'Perfect Magistrate,'" 287.
70. Ibid., 297.
71. Cissie Fairchilds, *Domestic Enemies: Servants and Their Masters in Old Regime France* (Baltimore: Johns Hopkins University Press, 1984), 168.
72. Gonthier, *Le châtiment du crime*, 163.
73. Andrews, *Law*, 77.
74. Gonthier, *Le châtiment du crime*, 161; on protection of small children, see also 34. The state and church severely punished women engaged in infanticide or any actions that could endanger the life of a child, but also opposed those who tried to limit married women's procreative activities. Witenne van de Walle, "The Decline of French Fertility," in *Family and Sexuality in French History*, ed. André Burguiére, Robert Wheaton, and Tamara Hareven (Philadelphia: University of Pennsylvania Press, 1980), 141.
75. Soman, "Sorcellerie, justice criminelle et société," 206, 205.
76. Barbara B. Diefendorf, "Widowhood and Remarriage in Sixteenth-Century Paris," *Journal of Family History* 7, 4 (1982).
77. Andrews, *Law*, 77.
78. Gauvard, *"De grace especial,"* 830.
79. Geremek, *The Margins*, 15, 49.
80. Chiffoleau, *Les justices*, 162; Schnapper, "Les peines arbitraires," 268. On death sentences for thievery, see also Bauchond, *La justice criminelle*, 205. Hanging was recorded since the twelfth century: Bauchond, 258.
81. Chiffoleau, *Les justices*, 238.
82. Ibid., 239; on types of executions see also Fouret, "Douai," 8; Langbein, *Torture*, 27-28.
83. Chiffoleau, *Les justices*, 162. One might add that amputation was widespread in the Muslim world.
84. Gonthier, *Le châtiment du crime*, 146.
85. Cristiane Plessix-Buisset, *Le criminel devant ses juges en Bretagne aux 16e et 17e siècles* (Paris: Editeur Maloine, 1988), 158.
86. Geremek, *The Margins*, 16.
87. Langbein, *Torture*, 40.
88. Geremek, *The Margins*, 16.
89. Ibid., 39.
90. Andrews, *Law*, 290.
91. Coopland, "Crime and Punishment," 79.
92. Cohen, "Violence Control," 120.
93. Boca, *La justice*, 180, 181; Bauchond, *La justice criminelle,* 208, 258-59; Geremek, *The Margins*, 15.
94. Boca, *La justice*, 217, 219.
95. Pierre Van der Vorst and Laurent Labruyerre, *A l'enseigne de la braconne: le parfait petit braconnier: bracinnages, braconneaux et braconniers, hier et aujord'hui* (Bruxelles: Editions de l'Université de Bruxelles, 1982), 231.
96. Farr, *Authority*, 19.
97. Pearl, *The Crime*, 95.
98. David Teasley, "The Charge of Sodomy as a Political Weapon in Early Modern France: The Case of Henry III in Catholic League Polemic, 1585-1589," *Maryland Historian* 18, 1 (1987): 26.

99.   Gonthier, *Délinquance*, 248; On the relationship between the sexual/political and social order see also Garnot, "La legislation et la repression," 76-77.

100.   Gonthier, *La châtiment du crime*, 311.

101.   Gauvard, *"De grace especial"*, 790.

102.   Boca, *La justice*, 191.

103.   Jeffrey Richards, *Sex, Dissidence and Damnation: Minority Groups in the Middle Ages* (London: Routledge, 1990), 30.

104.   Boca, *La justice*, 192.

105.   Gonthier, *Le châtiment du crime*, 130.

106.   Delumeau and Lequin, *Les malheurs*, 123.

107.   Gonthier, *Délinquance*, 313.

108.   Gonthier, *Le châtiment du crime*, 67.

109.   Jacques Rossiaud, "La prostitution, jeunesse et société dans les villes du sud-est au XVe siècle," *Annales* 31, 2 (1976): 300.

110.   Gonthier, *Le châtiment du crime*, 314.

111.   Cohen, "Violence Control," 117.

112.   Chiffoleau, *Les justices*, 236.

113.   Cuttler, *The Margins*, 118.

114.   Beatrice Gottlieb, "The Meaning of Clandestine Marriage," in *Family and Sexuality in French History*, ed. André Burgiére, Robert Wharton, and Tamara K. Hareven (Philadelphia: University of Pennsylvania Press, 1980), 60.

115.   Ibid., 60.

116.   Ibid., 58-59.

117.   Ibid., 60-61.

118.   Females over age twenty-five and males over thirty could marry without parental consent (Cummings, "Elopement," 118).

119.   Jacques Rossiaud, "La prostitution dans les villes françaises au XVe siècle," *Communications* 35 (1982): 83.

120.   Garnot, "La législation et la repression des crimes," 84.

121.   Farr, *Authority*, 94.

122.   Thierry Pech, "Foy et secret: le mariage clandestin entre droit et literature dans les Histoires de Boaistuau a Camus," *Société d'Étude du XVIIe siècle* 48, 4 (1996): 894.

123.   Madeleine Lazard, *Pierre de Bourdeille, seigneur de Brantôme* (Paris: Fayard, 1995), 215.

124.   Cummings, "Elopement," 223.

125.   Ibid., 121.

126.   Fairchilds, *Domestic Enemies*, 168.

127.   Gottlieb, "The Meaning of Clandestine Marriage," 65.

128.   Chiffoleau, *Les justices*, 107. On the drive against adultery in the fifteenth century, see Gauvard, *"De grace especial"*, 583; in the sixteenth century, see Boca, *La justice*, 79.

129.   Rossiaud, "La prostitution dans les villes," 83.

130.   Boca, *La justice*, 193, 192.

131.   Ibid., 220.

132.   Fouret, "Douai," 29; Maurice Level, "La repression de l'homosexualité," *Historama* 17 (1985) : 41. Garnot, *Crime et justice*, 126; on homosexuality: Chiffoleau, *Les justices*, 192.

133.   Geremek, *The Margins*, 15.

134.   Richards, *Sex, Dissidence and Damnation*, 117.

135.   J. L. Flandrin, "Repression and Change in the Sexual Life of Young People in Medieval and Early Modern Times," in *Family and Sexuality in French History*,

ed. Robert Wheaton, Tamara K. Hareven (Philadelphia: University of Pennsylvania Press, 1980), 31.

136. Geremek, *The Margins*, 87; Otis, "Nisi in Postribulo," 49.

137. Anne Terroine, "Le roi des ribauds de l'hôtel du roi et les prostitutuées," *Revue Historique de Droit Français et Étranger* 56 (1978): 254, 255, 262.

138. Geremek, *The Margins*, 92; Otis, "Nisi in Postribulo," 142.

139. Boca, *La justice*, 46.

140. Richards, *Sex*, 123, 125; on fifteenth-century France, see also Chiffoleau, *Les justices*, 186; Geremek, *The Margins*, 214.

141. Rossiaud, "La prostitution dans les villes," 69.

142. Richards, *Sex*, 125.

143. Ibid., 122.

144. Bauchond, *La justice criminelle*, 189-90, 209.

145. Gonthier, *Délinquance*, 325.

146. Barbara Beckerman Davis, "Poverty and Poor Relief in Toulouse, ca. 1474-ca. 1560: The Response of a Conservative Society" (Ph.D. dissertation, University of California, Berkeley, 1976), 456.

147. Mack P. Holt, "Order and Community in Sixteenth-Century Burgundy," *Proceedings of the Annual Meeting of the Western Society for French History* 16 (1989): 65.

148. Ibid., 123.

149. Erica-Marie Benabou, *La prostitution et la police des moeurs au XVIIIe siècle* (Paris: Libraire Académique Perrin, 1981), 21.

150. The connection between venereal disease and state control over sexual/social life can be seen in post-Soviet Russia. HIV/AIDS might "threaten the stability of the state, or force the state to enact draconian measures to contain the disease." Sarah E. Mendelson, Julie Sawyer, and Celeste A. Wallander, "The Security Implications of HIV/AIDs in Russia," Policy Memo 245, Center for Strategic and International Studies, Washington, DC, 2002, 1.

151. Farr, *Authority*, 139.

152. Riley, "Women and Police in Louis XIV's Paris," 40; A. Mericskay, "La prostitution à Paris dans les marges d'un grand livre,"*Histoire, Economie et Société* 6, 4 (1987): 496. One might add that there were attempts to provide poor women with outlets for gainful employment and other types of help to discourage prostitution; see Barbara Beckerman Davis, "Poverty and Poor Relief in Sixteenth-Century Toulouse," *Historical Reflections/Reflexions Historiques* 17, 3 (1991): 283; Raymond A. Mentzer, Jr., "Organizational Endeavour and Charitable Impulse in Sixteenth-Century France: The Care of Protestant Nîmes," *French History* 5, 1 (1991): 11-12.

153. Robert Descimon, "Les fonctions de la metaphore du mariage politique du roi et de la république de France, XVe-XVIIIe siécles," *Annales ESC* 6 (November-December 1992): 1134; Collins, "State Building," 605.

154. Descimon, "Les fonctions," 1135.

155. Neithard Bulst, "La lutte contre la peste noire en France (1348-début XVIe siecle)," *Bulletin d'Information de la Société de Démographie Historique* 36 (1985). One might add that the spread of the plague in the fourteenth century led to a proliferation of literature on plague. Alison Klairmont, "The Problem of the Plague: New Challenges to Healing in Sixteenth-Century France," *Proceedings of the Annual Meeting of the Western Society for French History* 5 (1977): 199.

156. Ronald Reid, *Paris Sewers and Sewermen: Realities and Representations* (Cambridge, Mass.: Harvard University Press, 1991), 92.

157. Trout, *City on the Seine*, 172.

158. Reid, *Paris Sewers and Sewermen*, 12.

159. Ibid., 88, 66.

160. Hilary Meg Ballon, "Architecture and Urbanism in Henri IV's Paris: The Place Royale, Place Dauphine, and Hopital St. Louis" (Ph.D. dissertation, Massachusetts Institute of Technology, 1985), 191. On cleanliness and disinfection in the sixteenth century, see also Jean-Noel Biraben, *Les hommes et la peste en France et dans les pays européens et méditerranéens*, 2 vols. (Paris: Mouton, 1975-1976), 2: 180.

161. Pierre-Denis Boudriot, "Essai sur l'ordure en milieu urbain a l'époque pré-industrielle: de quelques réalities écologiques à Paris aux XVII et XVIII siècles: les déchets d'origine artisanale," *Histoire, Economie et Société* 7, 2 (1988): 262.

162. Holt, "Order," 65.

163. Jean-Pierre Babelon, *Paris au XVIe siècle* (Paris: Diffusion Hachette, 1986), 289.

164. The first attempt to fight fire went back to fourteenth-century Paris. "As early as 1371 an ordinance had spelled out primitive measures to protect the capital—for example, compelling all persons to keep barrels of water at their doors." Trout, *City*, 222.

165. Herodotus, *The Histories*, 63.

166. José Barchilon, "Introduction," in Michel Foucault, *Madness and Civilization* (New York: Pantheon, 1965), vi.

167. Paul Dartiguenave, *Marginalité, déviance, pauvreté en France, XIVe-XIXe siècles* (Caen: Centre National de la Recharche Scientifique et du Centre de Recherches d'Histoire, Quantitative de Université de Caen, 1981), 21.

168. D. Bourrouilh and B. Cheronnet, "A propos de la peste en Béarn (1348-1652)," *Revue de Pau et du Béarn* 15 (1988): 49; Holt, "Order," 65.

169. Biraben, *Les hommes*, 2: 88, 102.

170. Ibid, 139.

171. Ballon, *Architecture*, 191; On the attempt to isolate the French cities from each other as the result of the plague see also Biraben, *Les hommes*, 2: 123.

172. Rossiaud, "La prostitution, jeunesse et société," 291.

173. Biraben, *Les hommes*, 2: 169.

174. Ibid.,176.

175. Ballon, *Architecture*, 195-96.

176. Babelon, *Paris*, 172.

177. Such extraordinary measures could also be seen in the future. They might not be as brutal, but they intruded on private life to a high degree and regulated personal activities to the smallest detail. In the 1918 influenza epidemic, Chicago authorities demanded arrest of "not only violators of the spitting ordinance, but every person found coughing or sneezing without using a handkerchief. All offenders caught will be taken directly into court." *New York Times*, October 4, 1918.

178. Delumeau and Lequin, *Les malheurs*, 265.

179. Otis, "Nisi in Postribulo," 98.

180. Biraben, *Les hommes*, 2: 118.

4

The Apparatus of Repression and Control

The study of the apparatus of repression and control can be divided into two parts. The first deals with the mechanism of direct repression. The role of the executioner was central as the direct agent of the state's terrorist endeavors. The second part focuses on the controlling and preventive elements of the apparatus—the evolution and proliferation of the police and judicial system.

Executioner as Profession

Historians and contemporary observers have widely explored the drama of the suffering of death, the spectacular aspects of executions. But few if any have paid attention to the fact that public executions, often accompanied by sophisticated tortures, were not just spectacles but professional work. They required more than a coldness or brutal insensitivity to human suffering, attributes not limited to executioners but found in occupations from soldiers to surgeons. Executioners also needed specific professional skills. The increasing employment of the death sentence and especially torture in dispatching criminals led to the emergence of executioners as a distinct professional group.

The image of the executioner was often distorted in the public's mind, and historians may have played a role in the creation of this image. Being an executioner can often be related to socially negative qualities. The best executioners had no sensitivities and in fact ceased to be human beings at all. A predilection for brutality made a perfect executioner. These negative characteristics made executioners similar to their social counterparts—violent criminals, rapists, etc. This image of the executioner was also deeply embedded in the terrorist practices of the numerous totalitarian regimes of the twentieth century. Since terror was an essential aspect of these regimes, the executioner was at the forefront and in many ways epitomized these societies. The executioner himself could be cynical, but the forces behind him were ideological or quasi-ideological. Tyrants, whether Stalin, Hitler, Mao, or Pol Pot, were driven by preconceived ideas of how to create an ideal society, as they fancied it, and, of course, by a desire for unlimited power. But most presentations of executions have ignored the fact that executions and hence executioners are not just products of a totalitarian society. They have been a part of Western democratic regimes for centuries. In some countries where capital punishment is still part of life, the USA, for instance, the executioner is also a part of society. Like any other representative of the law enforcement machine, the executioner needs to be a professional. This professionalism is part of the routine of the execution. It requires knowledge of psychology, how to control people and lead them to the execution site, and how to dispatch them according to the prescription of the law.

The professional role of the executioner was even greater in the early modern era when he was finally installed as a part of the judicial machinery. The importance of qualifications was due to the following: the job of the executioner in most cases was not just to dispatch the person but also to kill him or her through torture. The primitiveness of the tools of the trade was a premier problem. The job of the modern executioner is eased by the fact that machines do the job. The executioner in most cases needs to push the condemned into a gas chamber or fix him into an electric chair or onto a gurney.[1] In execution by shooting, the condemned is placed against a wall and the executioner needs only to pull the trigger; not much skill or physical force is required.

The situation was different in the past. Even beheading, one of the simplest methods of execution, required considerable strength to handle the heavy, broad-bladed sword that was the usual tool for it. Skill was required to avoid mishaps in which the head was not severed by one blow. These problems were complicated by the fact that in most cases the design was not just to dispose of the person but also to kill him or her in a specific way, to inflict the exact amount of suffering appropriate to the crime. Burning at the stake, quartering, and other types of torture required not only emotional insensitivity and physical strength but considerable skill. Executioners were often proud of their craft and developed the art of torture to a high level of perfection. Its goal was not only to terrorize the victim or instill in the minds of spectators the horrors of crime and its consequences, but also to provide visual instruction in the law. When intense torture was seen as unjustly administered, even the most insensitive observers felt sympathy for the victims.

To be torture, punishment must obey three principal criteria: first, it must produce a certain degree of pain, which may be measured exactly, or at least calculated, compared and hierarchized, death is a torture insofar as it is not simply a withdrawal of the right to live, but is the occasion and the culmination of a calculated gradation of pain: from decapitation (which reduces all pain to a single gesture, performed in a single moment—the zero degree of torture), through hanging, the stake, and the wheel (all of which prolong the agony), to quartering, which carries pain almost to infinity.[2]

The description of the law, the gradation of punishments, and the interpretation of the law required qualification, knowledge, and experience of all players in the judicial system. The executioner translated the judicial clauses into action. The gradation of torture and death was an essential aspect of the judicial system; it was to provide vivid instructions to the populace about the importance of various clauses of the law. In a twisted way, it played the same role in the judicial system of the ancien régime as today's books and lectures that translate complex multivolume collections of judicial wisdom into easily understood statements.

Appropriate punishment was also required due to the contractual nature of the exchange between society and the criminal. Society should be repaid in suffering comparable to the amount of harm the criminals had done to society. This strict application of the law and fine tuning in the gradation of punishment a requirement of the executioner's profession; he could be punished for inflicting not enough or too much pain.

The case of Robert-François Damien (1705-1757), the would-be regicide of Louis XV, illustrated that an inability to kill with the prescribed amount of pain made the executioner liable. The executioner, who was "unable to quarter his patient according to the rules, had to cut him up with a knife" (52). It was apparent that Damien had not received the amount of pain called for in the law. For this reason, the executioner was deprived of a bonus: "Damien's hair, which had been promised to him, was confiscated." The hair of a would-be regicide was an important artifact with perhaps some mystical value, so it had considerable market price. Confiscating it was a serious blow to the executioner. (The hair was sold and the proceeds used for charitable purposes.)

Excessive torture could also cause problems for the executioner, since a sense of legal impartiality was violated. An executioner in Avignon "caused excessive pain to three bandits, who were nevertheless formidable characters, whom he had to hang" (52). This pain, which, according to the law, these men did not deserve, bruised the crowd's legal conscience. They surrounded the scaffold, where there were not enough guards to protect the executioners and ensure the smoothness of the enterprise.

This incident seemed to be caused by the authorities' assumption that people were in full solidarity with the power that dispatched people who were a danger to society. Yet in this instance their views were not on the side of the authorities. The crowd considered that the pain inflicted on the criminals was legally wrong: it was more pain than they deserved. Viewing the criminals suffering unjustly, "the spectators became angry" (52). The crowd denounced the executioner and, "in order to punish him and also to protect him from mob violence, he was put into prison."

The profession of executioner was also a sort of family enterprise. Indeed, the job was passed from one generation to another. Children were trained from a young age to observe execution and torture. As they acquired experience and stamina, they started to assist their father in the trade. It was important to teach the youngsters to be insensitive to suffering.[3] Only children who were so trained could become brutal professional executioners.

The training of young Khmer Rouge soldiers for their future role as executioner/torturers is quite important to our story, for it provides insight into the training and emotional adaptation of the young would-be executioners in late medieval/early modern France.

> One of the most important objectives of Khmer Rouge training was to infuse the young cadres with callousness toward violence, pain, and killing. A key technique was the torture game. Animals, including domestic animals like dogs and monkeys, were systematically dismembered or burned by the children-soldiers. Prince Norodom Sihanouk, kept under house arrest during the Khmer Rouge period, witnessed these barbarities: Young recruits began "hardening their hearts and minds" by killing dogs, cats, and other edible animals with clubs or bayonets. Even after their April 17, 1975 victory, the Khmer Rouge kept in practice with a game consisting of throwing animals into "the fires of hell" since they had no human victims handy.... Another favorite was torturing monkeys, so much like humans in their reactions. Their balls were hacked off. They were chained by the neck and strangled as they ran behind their young captors, who pulled harder and harder at the chains. The screams of the poor beasts were heart-rending. The sight and sounds of them were unbearable. But the young Khmer Rouge youtheas [youths] couldn't get enough of it.[4]

This information from the Khmer Rouge provides the same insight into the training of executioners in the past as anthropological information about the life of indigenous people of some parts of the world (for example Amazon jungles) might provide insight into the life of people during the Stone Age. It is quite likely that French executioners trained their children in this way. In the process, the youngsters might help the parents. Wives engaged in helping their husbands in the trade. They were present at executions to provide encouragement and, if needed, help. In one case, as a victim tried to avoid hanging, the executioner pulled him from the ladder and "the wife of said executioner pulled at his feet from under the gallows."[5]

By the end of the fifteenth century there were qualified cadres of executioners. In Paris Jean Cousin, a man of great skill and great physical strength, once "struck so hard that '(Saint-Pol's) body hit the ground before his head.'"[6] Some provincial cities also had full-time executioners. From the fifteenth century d'Abbeville had a full-time executioner who received both a permanent salary and fees for each execution.[7] The fees were apparently to encourage him to be active on the job. The executioner had assistants to escort the condemned man to the place.[8] Executioners soon developed into dynasties, and the father transmitted his sword, the symbol of social status, in the same manner as the nobles.[9] By the fifteenth century, executioners started to wear a uniform. Parts of this uniform were given to them as payment for their work. A certain Denis Lepage in 1447 "received four pairs of gloves for having executed some soldiers.... Presumably the gloves were to protect his hands in the course of all judicial killing that he was doing."[10]

The executioner was a central figure in fighting asocial drives as well as various forms of social discontent. But he was only the final player in the system. The criminal had first to be apprehended and a verdict passed. Here lies the importance of the judicial machinery: the police and the court. These institutions existed in rudimentary form during the Middle Ages and started to increase in size and complexity by the beginning of the modern era. This development made the work of the executioners more effective.

The Emergence of the Police

Criminality, asocial behavior in general, was one of the most important characteristics of early modern society, so it was not surprising that the police started to emerge as a permanent force. They began to penetrate various aspects of life, and their presence marked the emergence of an absolutist state that could be seen as a police state.

Indeed, police and policing provided absolutist regimes with a similarity to the totalitarian states of the future. There were substantial differences, but in both cases there was a watch over personal behavior and pressure to regiment personal life. In early modern Europe there was much more stress on personal behavior. Morality, hard work, and religious values were essential for society, so preventing crime and other asocial processes received a great deal of attention. France was the classic example of the absolutist regime, and the development of the

French policing mechanism indicates the pattern of development that became common throughout most of Europe. The police focused on the prevention of crime. Indeed, security considerations integrated into the developing police system influenced all aspects of social life from politics to architecture.

Security Arrangements and Architecture

The concern with security could be seen in the architectural arrangements of the Middle Ages.[11] Medieval/early modern Europe had scenery dotted with grand castles. However, neither amenities nor comfort nor aesthetic considerations defined most construction in this period. Security was the primary consideration, with the result that formidable fortresses dominated much of Europe by the fifteenth century.[12] Security was important not only for nobles in the countryside, but for city residents as well. Architectural and social life were defined by security considerations, and the assumption that architecture was first of all to address security was certainly not imaginary. The experience of several generations of Frenchmen and other Europeans showed clearly that only those who were protected by a wall or lived in a fortified house could survive conflicts like the Hundred Years War.[13] So it is not surprising that architectural arrangements of the city were also in many ways defined by security. The best real estate was inside the wall. The wall created many problems. Space was limited, so the buildings were built many stories high. The streets were narrow with little light and poor sanitation. But the major concern was security, and the people were ready to tolerate inconvenience for that reason.

While living inside the wall was much more secure than living outside, it still did not guarantee security. The buildings inside the wall often were of castle type construction, even in Paris, the stronghold of the king, where security should be the highest. "As late as the fifteenth century, owners were still building prominent turrets (*tourelles*) on the frontages or the curtain wall of their hotels, often on the street corners."[14] Even a Parisian bishop did not feel that he was secure inside the city wall. "The Hotel de Sens (1475-1507), built as a Paris residence for the bishops of Sens, was in the vanguard of hotel design.... It was apparently designed to be defended, and the outer wall was pierced with small, irregular windows." Weapons hung on the walls, not as decoration but for practical reasons. They must be available immediately in case of attack.

"Insulation within the walls and control of passage through the gates also appeared to curb any threats to public order."[15] The city was concerned not only with the breakdown of social order and the spread of crime inside the wall, but also with the threat of attack from outside. Whether troops or bandits, they posed a threat of pillage and murder. This was the major reason walls were an essential part of a city's architectural design. "The community's right to self-defense was given tangible expression in the town wall. Walls surrounded even the humblest villages, and a stranger reaching a town was obliged to make his entry through a gateway fortified with drawbridge, portcullis and tower. The ramparts bristled with look-outs and crenellated battlements, and were girded with a protective ring of ravelins and moats."[16] "Seen from a distance the towns looked wholly enveloped in their walls, with only church steeples and in some cases the keep of the citadel peering above the fortifications." "The ramparts appeared to guarantee security against the external enemy, and to assure public order within."[17]

Security also defined the dress code. A sword or similar weapon was important for its symbolic value (demonstrating that a person was a free man and equal to nobles),[18] but it also had other uses. Weapons were double-edged, so to speak, to attack or defend. Many people carried arms because they could be attacked at any moment.

The sword attached to the belt and the formidable fortifications were essential in protecting the city both from foreign armies and from bandits, but fortifications alone could hardly provide total security. The mechanism of law enforcement was especially needed during the time marked by the proliferation of crime, the late Middle Ages.

The Development of the Apparatus of Law Enforcement

While crime increased, late medieval society still sought solutions to the problem in traditional arrangements. Medieval society was based on a *Gemeinschaft* culture of solidarity. Consequently, this was the way these societies tried to maintain control and check crime. The principles of *Gemeinschaft* society were holistic in the sense that to various degrees all members shared them.

A person did not exist on his or her own but was part of the group, and the group was responsible for all behavior, including the misbehavior of individual members. "Under the procedure known as frankpledge, every adult male was enrolled in a group of ten adults, called a tithing."[19] If an accused person failed to appear before the court, his tithing became responsible and, since most of the punishments consisted of fines, the tithings paid the fines.

There were attempts to cling to these familiar principles of social interaction to check criminal behavior even when this society started to erode, but they did not work. The weakness of the medieval king as maintainer of order was manifested in the weakness of the judicial system, which became dysfunctional at an early date. Historians maintain that "at the turn of the thirteenth century the sanctions of the common law were ineffective in curbing violence and corruption"; the kings themselves admitted that "laws were not at all well kept,"[20]—that traditional medieval systems of law enforcement did not work. The weakness of the state and proliferation of crime led to a popular response as all groups of society looked for a way to ensure basic security. Quite a few inhabitants sought security in the old *Gemeinschaft* arrangements from neighbors and kin rather than the weak or nonexistent institutions of the state. And social bodies continued to provide the major protection against criminals.

The elite led society in establishing a values system and a way of social interaction. Consequently, as asocial drives increased, the elite attempted to check antisocial proclivities, among the populace and in their own ranks, and tried to solve the problems in the context of the old models. "Lords formed transitory alliances to subdue rivals who broke the peace; and Peace Leagues took the field against robber barons."[21]

The church added its authority to help the nobility maintain order. The church itself was infested by crime and in some instances provided cover for criminals, but it was not completely criminalized. As a whole, the church was on the side of order, trying to help the elite. The "clergy proclaimed days of peace and tried to exempt certain places and people from violence." The masses were also anxious to find protection against the rising tide of criminality. There was little consolation in the fact that criminals were often from their own ranks.

The desire for order came from both the elite and other groups. It would be wrong to assume that in early modern Europe the social arrangement consisted of the oppressors (the elite and bureaucracy who used order as a form of oppression) on one side of the social barricade and, on the other side, the oppressed masses who joined the criminals in the fight for liberation. It is true that in some cases the masses sided with the criminals, especially if these "social criminals" had special relationships with people in various locations. But in most cases bandits could be described as "real malefactors of rural society."[22] Like other members of society, the majority of peasants sought protection in traditional *Gemeinschaft* arrangements, and "Neighbors banded together into tithings and hundreds in England."[23]

The medieval *Gemeinschaft* control over criminals was based on a familial solidarity where people helped each other because they felt the obligation of blood, neighborhood, etc. This sense of personal ties was in continuous erosion and became more and more unreliable as time progressed. There was also a new aspect of criminality with which the old system could not deal. Old self-defense principles were designed to deal with individual criminals or comparatively small groups of bandits, not with well-trained and well-armed groups.

The criminality of the early modern era was qualitatively different from the earlier form. Large gangs of discharged mercenaries were actually quasi-armies and could be defeated only by a strong and well-organized force. Here a new apparatus of power emerged. The major difference in this new institution was that it was created by the ruler rather than by the fabric of society. It was placed above society, an embryonic police force. Thus, by the end of the era an institution that could be compared with the modern police emerged, though it was quite weak.

The emergence of the police force was deeply connected to changes in European society, mostly the rise in criminal behavior, which was qualitative as well as quantitative. The well-armed, well-trained gangs were often comprised of discharged mercenaries and similar detritus of society. They existed as a result of the erosion of the traditional societal relationships, which plucked people from their traditional settings and made possible the creation of both bands of criminals and police as an institution that could confront these bands.

The end of the interpersonal relationships of the classical Middle Ages transformed mercenaries into asocial bandits. Mercenaries could be hired and then released as the need for their services changed. Lacking attachment and the sense of belonging to the broad constituency of civic society (as would soldiers in modern Western society), these people lapsed into banditry. Hiring people whose allegiance was based only on pay provided groups whose services could be used against predatory gangs, for members of these institutions of law enforcement had allegiance to no groups, but only to the one who paid them: the king. This embryonic police force filled the major role of getting rid of numerous dangerous bands.

In this new social arrangement, the ability to hire personnel provided the royal power with the framework to set up a machinery of law enforcement and repression (two indistinguishable functions), but it took a long time to build this machinery. The state attempted to compensate for the slowness by several means. One was the application of the death penalty and torture on a large scale. Another was the prioritization of security areas. While sufficient policing of the entire realm was beyond the ability of the crown, the monarchy did attempt to provide a modicum of security in the most sensitive areas.

Of course, the security of the crown headed the list. Of major concern in France was the protection of Paris as capital of the realm. "The kings, for the best of all selfish reasons—self-protection and self-enrichment— took a hand in the administration of justice and police in their capital City."[24] In the high Middle Ages, the king's power was essentially limited to Paris and nearby territory. Thus for him to instill some sense of order in the rest of the country would hardly be possible. The first institution for maintaining order in Paris went back to the eleventh century. In 1032-1060 Châtelet and the office of *prévôt* (provost) of Paris was created.[25] Châtelet became "the principal seat of common-law jurisdiction under the French monarchy from the Middle Ages to the Revolution." The prévôt "had jurisdiction over matters of common law, both civil and criminal; judged appeals from all royal and seignorial courts in Paris; heard un-contested cases; and dealt through notaries with proceedings anywhere in the kingdom." "The Provost of the Merchants, a civic as a distinct from a royal administrator, also operated a police service. The monarchy's was by far the more effective. So, when Henri I appointed Stephanus in 1032 (he died six years before the Battle of Hastings, 1066), the genesis of the Prefect of Police of Paris can be discerned."[26] By the 1254 the knight watch (*guet*) was fully institutionalized under the command of the *chevalier du guet*.[27] During the reign of Philip IV the Fair (1285-1314), in April 1301, the position of commissaire was institutionalized. These became the major executives of Châtelet to maintain law and order in the city. By approximately the end of the fourteenth century, "Security in Paris was principally the concern of the sergeants of the *Châtelets*, that is of those who executed the justice of the provost. They were divided into two detachments, foot and horse. The former carried out decisions and saw to security inside the walls, while the latter fulfilled the same functions outside, throughout the whole of the provost jurisdiction."[28] In March 1498, the judicial/police power of the Châtelet was concentrated in the hand of a "lieutenant civil" and a "lieutenant criminel."[29]

For the king, preservation of order in the court was even more im-portant than in the capital. By the thirteenth century there were special law enforcement bodies to ensure the tranquility of the court. "Law and order at court was kept by a *prévôt*, assisted by three lieutenants and 30 archers."[30] The fact that the king thought it necessary to place a strong police force in the midst of the court demonstrated clearly the infestation of crime in the society. Even the court was not free from violent crime.

The law enforcement system in Paris underwent considerable strengthening at the beginning of the fourteenth century. During the reign of Charles VI, the law enforcement agencies were centralized. "The provost of Paris's position continued to grow while the Châtelet was being organized. The evolution can be dated to 1320."[31] The role of the Châtelet was increased in 1389. "From this date through the ordinance of November 29, 1407, the provosts' powers were repeated and increased." The provincial cities also engaged in building a law enforcement apparatus. From 1345 the city of d'Abbeville had "sergents"—guards selected from among residents in good standing. By the fifteenth century their numbers were increased to eight.[32] By the fourteenth century there were also guards in other French cities.[33]

By the end of the sixteenth century the royal authorities had taken an additional step in building a law enforcement institution in Paris. In May 1526, a new office was attached to Châtelet. The role of the new officials was to find and arrest "murderers, vagabonds and people of bad life."[34] In 1572, Charles IX instituted the Bureau de Police, comprised of judicial officials and representatives of the city's middle class.[35] In May 1586 the work of the commissaires was made more efficient by attaching each of them to a region of the city.[36] To assist law enforcement in monitoring criminals and to increase general comfort, there were attempts to provide the streets with some lighting at night. There were ordinances in regard to this in 1504, 1558, and 1594.[37]

Implementation of a centralized police was coupled with solidification of the centralized apparatus of the state. The French centralized state was solidified by the seventeenth century. At that time, "Cardinal Richelieu (1585-1642) enormously expanded the administrative capacity of the state by creating the intendant, an appointed official paid by the king to maintain order, administer justice, and collect taxes in France's thirty-two provinces (géneralité)."[38] Police structure reinforced the basic structure of administrative order. In 1667 a specialized deputy for law and order, the lieutenant general of police, was created in Paris. By the end of the century, the practice had spread all over France and "there were lieutenants general in all major cities.

The government at first had limited resources, and for this reason concentrated on protecting the major cities. By the end of the Hundred Years War it began to bring order to the provinces. By the fifteenth century the government started to seriously address rural banditry.

The authorities also tried to find ways to avoid problems with mercenary soldiers. One method involved directing the flood of demobilized soldiers away from the home country. France was not unique in this respect, and some European countries "found a brilliant solution to the problem of demobilization: mercenary armies from abroad were hired to fight wars and then discharged outside the borders after the war."[39] This was only a partial solution, but, "although some of the troops still plundered as they were demobilized, the related problems never reached large proportions." Another way of solving the problem was disbanding armies step by step. After the Hundred Years War, France "never demobilized soldiers in sufficient magnitude to induce banditry." But this method was inefficient, and the state emphasized more and more the institution of the police, designed specifically for dealing with soldiers who became bandits. This institution also provided prompt and brutal punishment for apprehended culprits.

The king's army became both the source of the problem and a tool for its solution. On one hand, the growing army was an endless source of banditry. On the other hand, the army or semi-military units were the major law enforcement agency of the king in the countryside. "By the end of the Middle Ages, the king had established the principle of a standing army under royal command."[40] This army was used not only for expanding territory and protecting the country from invasion by foreign troops, but also for maintaining order in the country. It could be used not only against social and political discontent (peasant uprisings and noble revolts) but against purely criminal outbursts such as banditry. Already by the end of the fifteenth century "the fight against marauders, the soldiers without an army who became vagabonds, was intensified."[41]

Since the bandits were often runaway soldiers, fighting banditry was related to the problem of policing the army. Over the sixteenth century the government found it necessary to create a special force to tackle this problem. The origins of the rural police that roamed the countryside can be traced to the dawn of civilization. In classical Athens there was the institution of *ephebes*, "young warriors who took up the shield and spear to patrol the countryside."[42] The experience of history, of course, was forgotten by the beginning of the modern era, and the European states started everything from scratch.

One of the first institutions of this sort emerged in England. As time progressed, this mechanism of state control and policing of the countryside became a permanent body. "John II (1350-1364) created a large military force to patrol the highways and suppress the marauding bands of unemployed knights, foreign mercenaries, and army deserters who pillaged the land."[43] The role of these bodies expanded over time. "Their responsibilities grew to encompass suppression of crime generally on the king's highway."

The French king followed suit. François I in 1544 created the force called maréchaussée.[44] "The maréchaussée, the military police from which the Gendarmerie Nationale is directly descended, may be traced perhaps with a little imagination, to the elite warriors, the gens d'armes, the 'men-at-arms' who formed the king's bodyguard in battle."[45] By the beginning of the fifteenth century there was a rudimentary military police, the precursor of the future maréchaussée.

> The name *maréchaussée* derives from the fact that the military police in medieval times were under the marshals (*maréchaux*) of France, commanders of the royal armies. At the outset they answered to a single provost but as the numbers and missions multiplied, it became necessary to have several provosts, operating under a provost-general. A Constable (military commander-in-chief) of France, Arthur III of Brittany, brought the military police up to substantial numbers in 1439, when fifteen mounted companies were formed. In 1448, the infantry was added to the provost troops.[46]

Originally the military police dealt exclusively with the soldiers, but as time progressed its function increased. By 1536 the king gave the military police powers to deal with all crime committed on the road. By 1544 the *maréchaussée* was finally institutionalized as the rural police with broad functions. The prévôts emerged as rural police officers with the right of summary justice. "The duties it entailed were set out in a variety of edicts dating from the reigns of Francois I and Henri II, as well as the Edict of Roussillion issued in August 1564.... According to the edicts, officers of the *prévôt* such as the provosts, vice-bailiffs and vice-seneschals were expected to have charge of the countryside at all times, 'to keep it free of vagrants and soldiery...and to make the high roads safe for trade and travelers'"[47]

Through these institutions the government solved two problems at once. First, it now had a quasi-military police force to deal with banditry and discipline in the army. These institutions made the army easier to use for both military and police roles, for without discipline the army as police force could be quite limited. "Such an army had to have an internal police element for its own better governance, a provost corps, and, given the unsettled and dangerous conditions of the age, the king extended the scope of the military police to include the protection of his subjects in the rural areas and along the main roads."[48] Second, besides fighting banditry, the rural police were entrusted "to ensure that people respected the law which forbade private citizens to bear arms."[49] The prévôt had unlimited power over bandits caught red-handed. "Their proceedings were typically swift and informal." The culprits were promptly hanged "on the nearest tree."

Security of travel was related to good road conditions. "In 1599, the king created a centralized administrative authority to regulate all road- and riverways (*voirie*) in France. It was directed by Maximilien de Bethune (1559-1641), the Duke of Sully, who served as both the *Grand Voyer* of France and the *Voyer* of Paris." Various regulations were installed to secure the safety of the roads from the engineering point of view. [50]

The development of law-enforcement apparatus was slow, and the machinery of policing and control was far from efficient. There were several types of problems. First, the power of the French king was not absolute. His implementation of a unified police and judicial system was limited by traditions inherited from medieval times. Second, the complicated judicial system devoted itself not only to maintaining order but also to enriching its members. Third, the king looked to the sale of hereditary judicial offices to replenish revenue. All these issues hindered police effectiveness. Still, the tendency was to embrace control of all aspects of French society.

The police were not necessarily the product of a centralized bureaucracy. As civil societies emerged, the tradition of self-government became stronger in areas outside the center, and local police were responsible for maintaining order. These local police were incorporated into the social body of civil society. They had the characteristics of the police of absolutist states, such as a tendency to control and supervise all aspects of human life. Even in countries where the police force was not centralized and state-run, local police bodies assisted the state machinery. They worked together to create order and security, even at the expense of personal freedom.

Private police first proliferated in England. The North American colonies followed in establishing a police force, based on local support, which was integrated into the strong civil society that emerged almost immediately in the New World. "Public policing came to the United States with the first settlers. New Amsterdam, later New York, created a burgher watch in 1643, one year after it was founded."[51] The system was based on local civic responsibilities, for the first policemen were not paid until 1712. Soon "Constables, marshals, and watchers were appointed or elected in every settlement, with early recognition that payment was required to ensure effective performance." As a result, the comprehensiveness of control undoubtedly rose. "The expansion of public police forces has produced a genuine increase in police capacity in two ways: through more intensive and coordinated coverage of territory and through qualitative upgrading of personnel."[52]

However, the police as a product of civil society rather than of the centralized state was a limited phenomenon in the early modern era. In most cases the police were the product of the of the absolutist state, an essential aspect of the rising bureaucratic machinery, created from above to ensure control and security. This machinery apprehended criminals and delivered them to the executioners. Execution was the culmination of the judicial process. The goal was not only to eliminate the culprit, but also to provide incentives to others not to follow the road of crime.

Notes

1. Lethal injection has become popular in China, partly to avoid international criticism for being brutal and "uncivilized," and partly because it is cheaper and simpler than shooting. This method made it possible to exceed modern records for sheer numbers of executions, up to 10,000 in 2001, for example. Graig S. Smith "In Shift, Chinese Carry out Executions by Lethal Injection," *New York Times on the Web*, December 2001.
2. Foucault, *Discipline and Punish*, 33 (citations in parentheses in the text).
3. Similarly, sons of nobles hunted from an early age. Hunting big game not only provided a chance to build muscles and acquire skills, but killing animals instilled in the youngsters a psychological numbness toward the suffering of others.
4. Arch Puddington, "Pol Pot in Retrospect," *Commentary* (April 1987): 53.
5. Foucault, *Discipline and Punish*, 64.
6. Cuttler, *The Law*, 227.
7. Boca, *La justice*, 45.
8. Ibid., 48.
9. Gonthier, *Le châtiment du crime*, 156.
10. Cuttler, *The Law*, 35.
11. Gonthier, *Le châtiment du crime*, 59.
12. Jean Gallet, "En Bretagne seigneurie et pouvoir militaire du XVIe au XVIII siècle," *Revue Historique des Armées* 1 (1985): 5.
13. Braudel, *The Identity*, 2: 160-61.
14. Anthony Sutcliffe, Paris: *An Architectural History* (New Haven, CT: Yale University Press, 1993), 9.
15. Geremek, *The Margins*, 21.
16. Yves-Marie Berce, *History of Peasant Revolts: The Social Origins of Rebellion in Early Modern France* (Ithaca, NY: Cornell University Press, 1990), 10.
17. Geremek, The Margins, 21.
18. Norman J. Wilson, "Conceptions of Poor Relief in Sixteenth-Century Strasbourg," *U.C.L.A. Historical Journal* 8 (1987): 7.
19. Weisser, *Crime and Punishment*, 92.
20. Bellamy, *Crime*, 4. 6.
21. Bayley, *Crime*, 33.
22. Barkey, *Bandits*, 21.
23. Bayley, *Crime*, 33.

24. Philip John Stead, *The Police of France* (New York: Macmillan, 1983), 13.
25. Arlette Lebigre, "La naissance de la police en France," *L'Histoire* 8 (January 1979): 6; "Chatelet," *Encyclopedia Britannica Online*.
26. Stead, *The Police*, 13.
27. Lebigre, "La naissance de la police en France," 6.
28. Geremek, *The Margins*, 23.
29. Lebigre, "La naissance de la police en France," 6.
30. Knecht, *French Renaissance Monarchy*, 74.
31. Gauvard, "Fear of Crime," 29.
32. Boca, *La justice*, 44.
33. Gonthier, *Le châtiment du crime*, 59.
34. Lebigre, "La naissance de la police en France," 6.
35. Paolo Piasenza, "Opinion publique, identité des institutions, 'absolutisme': le problème de la légalité à Paris entre le XVIIe et le XVIIIe siècle," *Revue Historique* 290, 1 (1993): 102.
36. Lebigre, "La naissance de la police en France," 6.
37. James L. McClain, John M. Merriman, and Kaoru Ugawa, eds., *Edo and Paris: Urban Life and the State in the Early Modern* (Ithaca, NY: Cornell University Press, 1994), 151; see also Babelon, *Paris*, 292.
38. Bayley, *Crime*, 30-31.
39. Barkey, *Bandits*, 5.
40. Stead, *The Police*, 13.
41. Geremek, *The Margins*, 41.
42. Victor Hanson, *The Wars of the Ancient Greeks* (London: Cassell, 1999), 66.
43. Bayley, *Crime*, 30.
44. Claude Quetel, *De par le roy: essai sur les lettres de cachet* (Paris: Privat, 1981), 113.
45. Stead, *The Police*, 22.
46. Ibid., 23.
47. Berce, *History*, 69.
48. Stead, *The Police*, 13.
49. Berce, *History*, 69.
50. Ballon, *Architecture*, 4, 5.
51. Bayley, *Crime*, 32.
52. Ibid., 98.

5

Education and Reeducation of the People: Execution as Actor, Teacher, and Priest

As discussed previously, the state institutionalized a variety of torturous deaths as punishments for crime. The state had also created the machinery of repression, starting with the executioner, to implement these brutal punishments. The rationale for the punishments went far beyond the mere dispatching of criminals. Other kinds of execution would have been much more efficient. But the elaborate methods of torture cannot be explained, as do Foucault and other postmodernist historians, as merely the symbolic act of mastery over the body of the criminal. Although there was a symbolic aspect to the executions, it was integrated into the practical desire to eradicate crime.

European rulers' broad use of torture was not unique or in any way a special predilection toward cruelty. It was the only way to maintain an increased sense of order. So when the judicial machinery regularly dispatched many people, the representatives of this machinery assumed that the executions were to have a practical effect. They were to instill the rest of the population with the fear of crime and respect for the law, in the broad holistic meaning of the word. These pragmatic considerations defined the organization and display of punishment. There were several essential elements.

First, a maximum number of people needed to be present. Second, observation of the executions should have a positive effect on the public and instill the most appropriate ideas (from the point of view of the authorities). These tasks were accomplished in several ways. Natural curiosity and desire to be entertained would lead people to attend executions and be instructed by the sight of death, even including some who saw criminals as role models that defied authority. To instill observers with appropriate thoughts to lead them away from crime, the authorities designed two methods: orchestration of the punishment, in most cases extremely brutal with torture as an essential element, and the direct involvement of the church. The presence of the church was not primarily out of concern for easing the suffering of the condemned or the salvation of his or her soul (albeit this should not be ignored). Rather, it made execution similar to a religious service and upheld the sacredness of social and political institutions and norms.

Execution as Spectacle and Teacher

The educational aspect of executions was important because the state still had limited means of conveying messages to the general public. Early modern France had no movies or television, or even modern newspapers. Circulation of messages was limited to church services, announcements on the square, and public executions. Thus a major reason for public executions often accompanied with long torture was to have an impact on the public: to convince those who could be tempted that the benefits of crime could not compete with losing their lives in a horrible way and to instill all residents of France with awe before the law and social order. The religious, moralizing aspect of this social order was invariably enmeshed with legal discourse. Thus, the execution, in a twisted way, upheld the validity of religion and its moral standards. The religious aspect was also designed to prevent the executions' evolution into a sort of free spectacle, at least for some observers.

Execution as Teacher of Obedience

The authorities assumed that many if not most attendants, regardless of their original intentions, would be horrified and deterred from crime. For this reason, the organizers of the execution wanted a maximum amount of people to see the importance of morality and law. There were several designs to ensure this.

To start with, there was coercion to push the populace to observe an execution. The sight of an execution was definitely not pleasant, and many of those who came left after the beginning, not desirous of seeing the entire procedure from start to finish. But whether people wanted to see the procedure was not the point. They needed to see the execution and especially the macabre proceedings of torture and dismemberment. They also needed to see the corpse, sometimes mutilated and dismembered. The educational aspect explained why all these procedures took place in public places such as the square, major roads and other places people visited for their needs, where they would see the results of the work of justice, even against their will. The purpose was to instill people with fear of the wrath of the authorities.

This practice would continue into the era of the French Revolution, and spread from Western Europe to Russia during the Bolshevik Revolution. Lenin, for example, insisted on public display of his executions, his repressive machinery. Responding to one peasant uprising, he issued the following order:

Comrades! The insurrection of five kulak districts should be *pitilessly* suppressed...

1. Hang (and make sure that the hanging takes place *in full view of the people*) *no fewer than one hundred* known kulaks, rich men, bloodsuckers.

2. Publish their names.

3. Seize *all* their grain.

4. Designate hostages.... Do it in such a fashion that for hundreds of kilometers around the people might see, tremble, know, shout: *they are strangling* and will strangle to death the bloodsucking kulaks.[1]

If people were not eager to see the execution, the Bolshevik authorities compelled them to attend.

The same could be said of rulers in early modern Europe, who in some cases made presence mandatory at executions. Though pushing all types of people to observe executions, the authorities were mostly concerned with the educational aspect of executions for the simple folk and hoped that the executions would have a strong didactic underpinning.[2]

It was clear that in the minds of authorities all the people could be tempted to commit crime. They viewed all members of the human species as essentially animals. From this perspective, one could find that the political thought of the early modern era contained an element of egalitarianism. Indeed, Hobbes's work made no difference between nobles and commoners. All people were essentially the same in regard to the animal instincts that defined their behavior.

Yet, despite their vision of society as a whole, judicial authorities were more concerned with the lower classes. This was especially the case in the sixteenth and seventeenth centuries when banditry, the major preoccupation of the nobility in earlier periods, subsided somewhat. In the minds of the authorities, the lower classes had the weakest sense of restraint and were to be drawn to the site of torture; their horror would prevent them from engaging in crime. For this reason, the authorities compelled the populace more than the representatives of the elite to observe the execution and torture. "People were summoned as spectators: they were assembled to observe erected in public squares or by the road side: sometimes the corpses of the executed persons were displayed for several days near the scenes of their crimes."[3] This was done apparently for only one reason: The sight would terrify society, especially the lower part of the populace. "Not only must people know, they must see with their own eyes. Because they must be made to be afraid."

Execution as Teacher of Revolt

It was often not necessary to enforce attendance, at least for all people. Organizers of executions could usually rely on the natural curiosity of some segments of the crowd, although this was not the only rationale. The desire to see death was due to various causes.

Executions did not always accomplish the purpose intended by the authorities—to instill the viewers with respect or fear of the law. Observing death could have the opposite effect: to teach people how to rebel against authorities, or at least how to face death. Execution could also serve as entertainment. In this case the state squandered its resources to provide free entertainment for the public. Yet with all the potential negative implications, the state still assumed the executions to be worthwhile arrangements and that the spectacle would deter the majority of people from engaging in criminal behavior.

Attraction of a crowd to the execution site was risky business from the perspective of the authorities. It is true that some of the condemned followed expectations. On the scaffold, they publicly acknowledged their wrongdoing, saw in the punishment their deserved suffering, and asked God to forgive them and their fellow criminals.[4] They almost thanked the authorities for taking the effort to apprehend them, torture them, and finally dispatch them—this cleansed their souls and provided them entrance into heaven. These people became the model for criminals who underwent *bonne mort*—the good death that created no problems for the authorities and provided, as expected, a beneficial influence on the spectators. The authorities were interested in increasing the numbers of condemned criminals who would exercise such an elevating influence on the public and justify the expense of elaborate torture and execution. And in the future a special collection of money would be launched with the explicit goal of encouraging the condemned to die with the message of repentance and piety.

At the same time, these exemplary condemned were far from a majority. In many cases the person on the scaffold behaved in a way that could hardly be pleasing to the authorities. This type of behavior included "defiant refusals to make death testaments; insults shouted at magistrates and the executioners; self-justifying appeals to the crowd; stoic endurance and mocking disdain of the suffering on the cross and wheel; and, most seriously, loud, dramatic spurning of the priest's exhortations and prayers."[5] The sight of brave and unrepentant criminals could plant rebellious thoughts in the minds of the common folk instead of discouraging them from wrongdoing.

Another complication for authorities was the fact that bystanders who watched the executions had different and often controversial feelings in regard to the criminals.[6] On the one hand, they could be pleased to see the criminal at the hands of the executioner, even though they might not have a developed a legal sense that the criminal was a social outcast who had broken the notion of the social contract and for this reason needed to pay. This notion was quite weak at the beginning of the modern era, affecting only a small segment of the urban population. But, especially if the executed were murderers or bandits who were not dangerous to everyone, bystanders might see the spectacle of their executions as the brave last stand of a hero who had fought against the hated authorities. They could be seen as martyrs who suffered because of injustice, as the public used the term, and it is clear that one reason the crowds appreciated the courageous behavior of victims on the scaffold was that tortured criminals exhibited a sort of rebellious defiance against the power of the king.

Those who came to see criminals were not just people who came to see a celebration of stamina and endurance; their observation of an execution had broader implications. Indeed, those who died courageously did not just demonstrate stamina and an ability to withstand suffering. These people did not confront abstract suffering; they confronted suffering inflicted by the state. It was suffering endorsed by the church. It was suffering inflicted by the authorities. Those who withstood this suffering actually confronted the authorities, and their stamina was a manifestation of opposition to the authorities. These implications were even stronger when they made statements that openly challenged the authorities and the church.

In fact, criminals had an extraordinary opportunity for political or religious confrontation with the regime. "The victim had an extraordinary, public freedom. He could stage his own death."[7] The reason for this was simple. "On the Greve, royal and ecclesiastical authority had little actual power over the condemned. He was going to die, only spiritual threats could restrain him from behavior, but penitential behavior could not be enforced on the unrepentant, the unbelieving, or the enraged. Here was the great paradox of the Old Regime execution: the actual power of state and Church over the condemned—the power as a measure by capacity to determine behavior—was at nadir inside the ritual of the execution."[8] As a matter of fact, the crowd that surrounded the scaffold implicitly expected that the great criminal (i.e., the leader of a large band) would behave in such a way, that he would brave suffering and defy the authorities.

Indeed, "If the crowd gathered round the scaffold, it was not simply to witness the sufferings of the condemned man or to excite the anger of the executioner: it was also to hear an individual who had nothing more to lose, curse the judges, the laws, the government and religion. The public execution allowed the luxury of these momentary saturnalia, when nothing remained to prohibit or punish. Under the protection of imminent death, the criminal could say everything and the crowd cheered."[9]

Execution as Entertainment and Teacher of Life

It is clear that a demonstration of rebellion on the stage of the execution bothered authorities more than anything else about the process. There were cases when people attended executions only to see defiance of authority. Yet these were not the major stimuli for people to attend, or at least they coexisted with the other reasons, equally unrelated to the authorities' major goal of instilling viewers with fear and respect for the law. Free entertainment was definitely the major reason many people flocked to the square where the action took place. In some cases, this desire to be entertained would combine with the fascination with a daring criminal, who by his daring exploits had defied the power of the king and the entire social and political order.

One reason for such an opportunity was that people in the pre-modern era had little entertainment available, even in big cities like Paris. Social gatherings with conversation and drinking were limited to comparatively small numbers of people, for daily travel even in Paris was no easy matter. At best these gatherings were limited to those who lived in the same neighborhood. Other forms of entertainment such as theater and reading required skills or money.

These forms of entertainment were also socially limited, for one can assume that access to the theaters patronized by the upper and middle classes would be impossible for poorly dressed members of the populace.

There was only one source of weekly entertainment: church attendance. Yet, even this diversion could not be seen as real entertainment. Entertainment implies relaxation, which implies uninhibited language, gestures, and ease to indulge in drinking, flirtation, and lovemaking, a need satisfied by the yearly fair or carnival but not the church.

Thus, cases when one could enjoy real entertainment were rare, and executions were among them. Executions as a spectacle were fully incorporated into the sadistic inclination of the culture and were in no way different from other sorts of entertainment enjoyed by the populace. "In Paris during the sixteenth century it was one of the festive pleasures of Midsummer Day to burn alive one or two dozen cats. This ceremony was famous. The populace assembled. Solemn music was played. Under a kind of scaffold an enormous pyre was erected. The sack or basket containing the cats was hung from the scaffold. The sack or basket began to smolder. The cats fell into the fire and were burned to death, while the crowd reveled in their caterwauling." The spectacle was attended not only by the lower classes: "Usually the king and queen were present. Sometimes the king or dauphin was given the honor of lighting the pyre. And we hear that once, at the special request of King Charles IX, a fox was caught and burned as well."[10] The French people followed a long tradition starting with the Romans, who widely used gladiatorial fights and public executions as a way of entertaining the crowd.

Other events that resembled executions were well known to the populace. These included theatrical performances at carnivals and fairs and the solemn pageants of the king's entry into the town and church processions. In fact, preparations for executions were staged in the same way as a solemn theatrical play. The solemnity, of course, lay in the fact that they were to demonstrate the triumph of the law. The condemned man was delivered to the place with special arrangements, in some cases "with sounds of trumpets."[11] The "horrors of the torture were quite spectacular."[12] It could be conducted in the daytime, but it might be conducted at night, under the light of torches. The theatrical aspect was especially strong in the execution of an important person.[13] In the provinces executions could be carried out "in some style, with the officials partaking of a large meal afterwards."[14] The feast related these events to carnival shows or theatrical performances. It confirmed executions' theatrical nature, at least in the eyes of many.

Indeed, executions were an exciting spectacle. They were real events, and no actor could compete with an actual death. They were full of unpredictable, exciting events that would be imprinted on one's mind forever. They could provide viewers with a good feeling that life, despite its miseries, was not so bad after all. Even the most miserable existence was better than a prolonged and painful death. They were also a sort of equalizer, for, similar to church services, people from all walks of life, from the upper echelons of the elite to commoners, attended. Indeed, lack of entertainment not limited to the lower classes: the upper classes could be just as bored.

Women lived in the same conditions as men and were among those who attended executions. The female soul could be as hard as the male. Indeed, one could say that the sentimentality of the legal culture of an emerging society, the charming smiles of the emerging modern legal order, concealed the natural Darwinism and essential cruelty.[15] Brutality was a prominent aspect of daily life in early modern Europe, France in particular. For this reason, ladies of the most delicate nature would see no reason why they could not enjoy seeing a criminal broken on the wheel and read a novel afterward.

Among the spectators in the eighteenth century were also members of the French academic world, who watched human suffering with the same indifference as the death of an insect. There was a recorded incident when one of these savants tried hard to be close to the object of observation and seemed to express a certain fascination with how the executioner had done his work. The executioner was apparently pleased by the attention and personally interceded on behalf of the savant, asking the other observers to show him a way to view an execution in detail. It is clear from this anecdote that attendance at executions did not degrade anyone, and the most humble visitors of the performance were aware that they would be in quite good company.

Additionally, attending executions required no payment. It was gratis entertainment. In fact, the death shrieks and groans could bring many kinds of pleasure to sadistic-minded observers, including sexual pleasure, especially if the victims were pretty women or handsome men.

Execution as Teacher of How to Die

While the entertaining aspect of death and violence and the opportunity to see defiance of the authorities were major reasons the populace often flocked to executions of their own will, there was another aspect of violence and death that attracted them: its educational aspect. In watching the executions, members of the French populace were instructed in the art of dying. There is no doubt that "plebeians lived in the omnipresence of death—by sickness, accidents, and violence."[16] For this reason, they were also looking for a way to accept death. To be sure, they wanted first to be entertained. Yet, if only at a subconscious level, they wanted some sort of instruction as to how to exit from life. They wanted to understand concepts that had been proposed to more educated persons in books and philosophical and existential treatises from Boethius (c. 480-c. 525) to Michel de Montaigne (1533-1592), who reiterated that the art of living was nothing but the art of dying.

Of course, the teachings of the church addressed this issue, and this was a major reason many people of every class clung to the institution. But people also needed practical examples, not only to accept the idea of leaving this world, but also to see how to withstand the most excruciating pain. For this reason, the French populace seemed to be "connoisseurs of stamina, courage, strength, and humor at deadly moments" (82). Undoubtedly for many of them this attitude indicated that they could stand the most prolonged suffering. The idea was comforting, and they were glad to see the executions, the "celebrations of life-force and lessons in the art of dying."

By watching the death of courageous and iron-willed criminals who withstood torture and faced death boldly, people came to the conclusion that one could endure the most horrible torture. At the same time the sight provided observers from all classes with the lesson that life is fragile and could end at any given moment, that death is the ultimate end of everyone.

All these considerations explained why the populace often attended executions of their own free will, and why they felt a "sadistic curiosity" and "fascination with dying" (81). The culprits who died on the scaffold often enjoyed popularity that could be compared to that of modern actors. This aspect of the populace's approach to criminals did not escape the attention of contemporaries. "There are cobblers who know the history of the hanged and their executions as thoroughly as men of cultivated society know the history of the kings of Europe and their ministers" (388).

Thus, people gathered around the scaffold for different reasons, often quite different from the intentions of the authorities. The authorities did not engage in the time- and money-consuming process of dispatching individuals though ritualized tortures because of sadistic proclivities. There was no desire to be symbolic in their actions, nor any special desire to engage in a display of the king's power, albeit it was definitely present in the arrangement. The authorities intended to instill observers with a respect for the social and political order. Taking into account the strong animal- type drive of most people, who had few internalized restraints and often were on the brink of starvation, there were very few ways to make the authorities' message persuasive. The major argument here was quite simple: A long, slow torturous death would break the will of the executed criminal and the sight would instill those horrors in the minds of the majority, regardless of the reasons that brought the majority of the people to the site of the execution.

Authorities believed that the majority of the populace would be horrified, despite indications that some were amused or encouraged to defy authority to the very end. But the horror could not achieve the desired effect unless moral authority supported the executions. The state thus defended the law, which had been transformed into a quasi-religion. The execution became both macabre theater and religious ceremony.

Torture as Spiritual Admonition

The reason to use the most brutal forms of execution was not rooted in some sort of peculiar "episteme" that had crept into the minds of the elite. Nor could it be explained in purely Marxist terms, as a way for the elite to maintain power and exploit the hapless populace, though this was one of the major considerations. The reason for the gruesome brutality was much deeper and broader. On the one hand, the state and the entire society faced a great drive for meltdown, a Hobbesian war of "everyone against everyone," and the state existed in a condition of continuous emergency. On the other hand, the techniques and apparatus of the state were in an embryonic stage. It had few resources and limited experience. So it was likely to act promptly, indiscriminately, and quite brutally. The wide application of terror was pragmatic, undertaken not only to eliminate problems quickly, but also to provide a deterrent for potential culprits. The use of terror was to provide the bystanders with easily comprehensible lessons that various actions, especially violent actions, could lead to a most macabre death. Precisely these reasons led the state to engage in expensive and time-consuming public executions. But the brutality of the punishment did not always have the intended effect on the bystanders; it could lead to an opposite result. Observers, especially of the lower classes, could celebrate the executed bandit, if he withstood torture and preserved his composure on the scaffold. The presence of the public could inspire the criminal or rebel to behave courageously and in turn inspire bystanders to follow in his footsteps.

This consideration was factored into the design of the authorities. Any defiance directly challenged the entire panopticon of moral structure and was to be prevented by all means possible. There was a reason why moralized metaphysics in the form of religion was incorporated into the proceedings. The design of the authorities was not only to maintain the sacredness of political and social order through the blessings of the church and underscore that the executions were not sheer manifestations of arbitrariness, but also implicitly to support the church and the religious values that were implicitly enmeshed in legal discourse.

The church was to be present at the site primarily to provide sanction for the execution, not to comfort the executed. If there was an element of comfort, it was not for humanitarian or meta-humanitarian (saving the soul of the condemned) but for utilitarian reasons. The placated and comforted victim would create less trouble, and this would facilitate an efficient performance. In this case, one could remember the well-known statement of Marx about religion as opium for the people. Religion played the same role as did the drugs given before execution in American prisons. The tranquilizer made the work of the executioner easier.

The religious aspects of death had other important implications. Religion was a force in itself. Its moral commandments and external symbols were interwoven with the social and political order and were the reason the king solemnly swore to uphold religion upon ascension to the throne. "I shall make every effort, and in good faith, to eliminate from my land from any jurisdiction subject to me all persons denominated 'heretics' by the Church" (81). No one could break the moral commandments of religion without risking the most brutal punishment. Religion was seen as the symbol of the divine and therefore social order. The rulers of early modern Europe would have agreed with Durkheim that "society is a religious phenomenon."[17]

Law as Religion: Implications for Punishment

Durkheim stated that there was a deep connection between religion and law and between the deep sacredness of religious maxims and social stability. He regarded the symbolism of religious rituals as essential to socialization. (Talcott Parsons supported this idea.)[18] While essentially valid, Durkheim's approach could not be applied to early modern Europe in its totality. In Durkheim's view, people's attachment to religion was a spontaneous result of their grassroots socialization. The situation was different in the early modern era. People believed in God and visited church on occasion. Yet this often had little if any implication for their daily activities, and religion often failed to instill in them any feeling of socialization, of following the norms of social interaction. The importance of religion as a form of restraint came not from below, but from above, from the state, which was primarily concerned with checking asocial behavior. This was the major reason the early modern state increased prosecution of crime against or disrespect toward religion.

The societal implications of the violation of religious doctrines were in the minds of the judges when they considered how to punish violators. Characterizing the attitude of sixteenth-century judges from Rouen, Jonathan Dewald stated that judges "were neither skeptical nor indifferent to religious crimes, but they dealt with them in the terms of other, to them more basic concerns: concerns about social ties and social order that flowed directly from their professional commitments."[19] The violation of particular rules endangered not only the social and political order in its particular form—the absolutist monarchy as the force that defended the interest of the elite—but also order in the holistic meaning of the word. And it was one of the major reasons in the Middle Ages and early modern era for European society's concern with religion. From the thirteenth century there were laws against those who engaged in blasphemy, and by the sixteenth century there was an "obsession with the blasphemy" in French judicial thought.[20] According to the rules, blasphemy was punishable by the mutilation of the tongue.

Ordinances were issued against blasphemy in 1510 (Grand Ordinance of 1510), 1514, 1546, 1572, 1581, and 1594. Most of these stipulated severe punishment for blasphemy and other types of crimes related to religion.[21] Cities such as Dijon imposed fines on those who engaged in "blasphemy, working on Sunday or feast days."[22] As the absolutist state increased its power, its concern for the "Ten Commandments" increased. As a result, there was a dramatic increase in prosecution of crimes against religion by the end of the sixteenth century. Church-related crimes such as theft from churches were punished with special severity.[23] In its drive for religious probity, the state often recognized little difference between children and adults, and "the child capable of committing sacrilege was treated as adult."[24] Both state and church saw this drive as "necessary to discipline the people."[25] Rigor and repression against forces hostile to religion were not only imposed from above, but also occasionally supported by the people from below. There were numerous cases of spontaneous lynching of people suspected of engaging in sorcery.[26]

As time progressed, religion became more and more interwoven with law, and was the essential justification for punishment. Torturous executions were done not because of the arbitrariness of the rulers, a sheer manifestation of power, but because the crime was an offense not just against the king but also against the Lord.[27] The king, a tool in the hand of divine justice, was to ensure the "maintenance of social and moral order," and "fight against Satan."[28] Those who offended the law and the king became a force on the side of the Prince of Darkness. This direct connection between religion and state was noticed by political thinkers. "The connection between the state and religion resembled the relationship between the body and soul."[29] Those who committed common crimes not only broke divine law but also committed high treason. The connection between common crimes and treason was quite clear in the judicial thought of the time.[30] Criminals violated political, social, and religious laws, all interconnected. They became not the enemy not just of society or even the king, but of the entire panopticon of the divine cosmos.

This deep integration of religion into the law (law as religion and religion as transmogrification of law) led to the vision that law enforcement authorities, especially judges as quasi-priests, should have high moral standing. This explains why the authorities fought against corruption and abuses of the power on the part of law enforcement agencies. A guard (sergeant) who abused his power could be sent to his death. In such a case the judges could apply arbitrariness to the punishment.[31] And it goes without saying that judges themselves were not immune from corruption. For this reason, by the sixteenth century, the most severe punishments would be inflicted on judges convicted of serious abuse of power, accepting bribes.[32] While judgeships could be bought, this could not be the case with verdicts.

Moreover, the quasi-priestly role of the judges and all representatives of power/law explains why those who abused these authorities, even verbally, could be severely punished. Piercing the tongue was done, at least in fifteenth- and sixteenth-century d'Abbeville, to those who spoke ill of king and magistrates.[33] Concern with the sacredness of an external display of religious symbols easily understood by the populace was a major reason for the deep integration of religious ceremony into executions. By the fourteenth century, a priest was usually present at the execution, and from 1397 he heard the confession of the condemned and provided symbols of reintegration of the condemned into the community of Christians.[34] This divinization of law and execution as the highest manifestation of its power also explained what seems to be a contradiction between the humanitarian aspect of religion and the brutal actions of the executioners. The moralizing dichotomies of Christianity were interwoven into the entire fabric of the procedure of execution.

While the condemned and the executioner climbed the ladder to the top of the gallows, "The priest climbed to a position just below the condemned, holding the crucifix before his eyes."[35] At that point, "the spirituality of the execution now reached its culmination. The priest gave final blessing and began chanting the Salve Regina. His song of mercy was joined in a rippling, mounting wave of voices by the entire population of the ritual at the Greve—judges, clerks, guards, crowd, executioner and condemned." This prayer, of course, was an expression of an essential aspect of Christian doctrine: that the living and the dead are one community in Christ. Yet the ritual was not just a spiritual tranquilizer that facilitated the act of the execution; it implied that the religious doctrine was implicitly connected to serious matters, that those who dared to trespass against legal and moral rules would be punished in the most severe way. The thinking was that criminals trespassed not only against the law, but also against the divine order. Law and religion were the same, and for this reason there was no way the criminal could escape the wrath delivered by the authorities--the priests of religion as law.[36]

The moral aspect of religion was a harbinger of death more than salvation, thus, "during the last verse of the *Salve Regina*, the executioner yanked the condemned into the air or, in breaking, struck the first blow with the rod" (81). It also explained why brutality was inserted into the last chants of prayer, as Christ was asked to save those "who are justly afflicted for our sins" (80).

The original religious exaltation of the condemned could be changed, and in his or her last moment (this indeed happened) he or she could make a blasphemous expression that spoiled the educational aspect of the entire enterprise. For this reason, the executioner minimized the time span between the last chant and the execution: "No profane time was to elapse between the ending of that communal prayer and the onset of dying. The priest continued to lead in prayer, directly below or beside the condemned through and beyond his agony" (81). The educational aspect of punishment, the reactivation of observers' piousness and moralizing restraint, was not to be compromised, and blasphemous uttering should be avoided by any means possible. This explained the occasional sign of "humanitarianism" in conducting the punishment.

"Humanitarianism" was often used in cases where there might be prolonged torture. The fear was that a person might not lose consciousness immediately after the first wave of acute pain and lapse into blasphemy or some other type of undesired cursing. For example, breaking on the wheel was among the forms of punishment that could have a different implication for displaying the might of the law and morality enmeshed in religion. "The Parliament customarily issued secret instructions, or retenta, for the executioner to strangle the victim rapidly with a leather garrot, that was attached to the cross and wheel" (77).

The same practices were used in burning, a punishment quite popular up to the last years of the ancien régime. Its popularity could be traced to the Middle Ages, when it was customary to burn heretics at the stake. As with the wheel, the pain could lead to undesirable curses, so "Virtually all burnings were also executed with retenta, for the same reason as with breaking. Just before the fire was started, the executioner either garroted the victim at the stake, inside the woodpile and beyond sight of the crowd, or thrust the pointed wood hook into his heart" (98).

These mercy killings were not purely humanitarian in nature. Of course, one could assume that all this was done for high spiritual reasons and a deep concern for a person's salvation. According to this interpretation, "Execution both extinguished a physical life and gave a salvational opportunity to a soul. Those who died blaspheming were doomed" (77). Yet, one might question whether this sort of humanitarian consideration was of paramount importance, or whether the real reason was quite different. "Retenta was issued for a spiritual reason: the pain of breaking and the wheel was intense, and easily provoked blasphemous curses that sabotaged the ministrations of the priest" (77). Discarding religion undermined the educational and indoctrinating aspects of the execution (the deadly seriousness of the moral religious commandments) and for this reason must be avoided by all means possible. In most cases the authorities did not expect the condemned to internalize guilt, to see in his or her imminent punishment the way to salvation and exhibit a willingness to follow the road of suffering. Yet, there were recorded instances when the condemned expressed such feelings.

Even some criminals understood this dissolving of the law into religion, the elevation of the law to the level of religious import, and saw their punishment as a quasi-religious purification. There were also recorded confessions at the moment of execution as a way of spiritual cleansing.[37] Some felt that by breaking the law they had not only trespassed against the temporal provisions of the authorities but also committed sacrilege. In this context the punishment was divine retribution, a way of cleansing the soul. This was the reason that, in order "to avoid eternal damnation" some criminals confessed in the "last moment" before the execution "even to the crime of bestiality, thus incurring death by burning instead of hanging, and the details were duly recorded."[38]

Notes

1. Martin Malia, "Lenin and the 'Radiant Future,'" *New York Review of Books*, 1 November 2001, 35.
2. Gonthier, *Le châtiment du crime*, 90-91.
3. Foucault, *Discipline and Punish*, 58.
4. Michel Bée, "Le spectacle de l'execution dans la France d'ancien régime," *Annales* 38, 4 (1983): 850.
5. Andrews, *Law*, 82.
6. Bée, *Le spectacle*, 843.
7. Andrews, *Law*, 82.
8. Ibid., 83.
9. Foucault, *Discipline and Punish*, 60.
10. Elias, *History*, 1: 203, 204.
11. Boca, *La justice*, 215, 214.
12. Soman, "Sorcellerie, justice criminelle et société," 197.
13. Gonthier, *Le châtiment du crime*, 189, 152.
14. Potter, *Rigueur de justice*, 269.
15. Albert Sorel elaborated on this, stating that the entire modern European culture was steeped in cynicism, seen especially in foreign policy. In his view, state interest, not morality, defined the course of action for most European states.
16. Andrews, *Law*, 81 (citations in parentheses in text).
17. Parsons, *The Structure*, 427.
18. Ibid., 417.
19. Dewald, "The 'Perfect Magistrate,'" 299.
20. Olivier Christin, "Sur la condamnation du blasphème (XVIe-XVIIe siècles)," *Revue d'Histoire de l'Église de France* 80, 204 (1994): 43, 47, 49; Schnapper, "Justice criminelle," 256, 278; Garnot, *Crime et justice*, 60, 62.
21. Garnot, "La legislation et la repression des crimes," 78.
22. Holt, "Order," 66.
23. Schnapper, "Justice criminelle," 256, 278-79; Gonthier, *Le châtiment du crime*, 180-81, 144. See also Gauvard, *"De grace especial"*, 944.
24. Schnapper, "Les peines arbitraires," 95.
25. Plessix-Buisset, *Le criminel*, 50.
26. Alfred Soman, "La decriminalisation de la sorcellerie en France," *Histoire, Économie et Société* 4, 2 (1985): 182.
27. Gonthier, *Délinquance*, 310.
28. Ibid., 324, 325.
29. Philippe Papin, "État et religion à la fin du XVIe siècle: de la vraye et legitime constitution de l'État," *Nouvelle Revue du Seizième Siècle* 8 (1990): 84; on the importance of religion for the stability of the state, see 86.
30. Cuttler, *The Law*, 54.
31. Schnapper "Les peines arbitraires," 94.
32. Plessix-Buisset, *Le criminel*, 204-5.
33. Boca, *La justice*, 221-22.
34. Boca, *La justice*, 215; Bée, "Le spectacle," 850, 852.
35. Andrews, *Law*, 80.
36. Equation of law with religion could also be seen in societies where the difference between law as temporal creation and religion or "divine" law was clear. Divine law commanded Antigone to bury her traitor brother, while state law prohibited it. Antigone's dilemma could be replayed on Russian soil as the author sided with

those who supported "divine" law. Dmitry Shlapentokh, "Antigona Valentina Rasputina," *Vozrozhdenie* 150 (1989).

37.   Gonthier, *La châtiment du crime*, 85, 192.

38.   Coopland, "Crime and Punishment," 84.

6

Dealing with Vagabonds: Repression and Social Engineering

In dealing with criminals, the state's first goal was to physically eliminate the most dangerous people. Second, the spectacle of gruesome torture
should deter potential criminals from engaging in wrongdoing. The state
in many ways followed the same strategy in dealing with vagabonds, seen
as potential criminals. Vagabonds were not harmless "proto-hippies," as
Foucault and his followers liked to portray them, or victims of a "bad
label" the emerging middle class applied to them; they were a real threat
to all classes of society. So the state tried to treat them as it treated criminals—remove them from society. At the same time the state's treatment
of marginals had specific features. The marginals were quite numerous
and the state tried to use them as slave labor or as material for various
state-sponsored projects, for example, populating the colonies. This use
of vagabonds was not so much a result of the emerging of the particular
episteme of capitalist society that required the people to be engaged in
productive labor as it was to other reasons.

The rise of state power provided the means for use of the vagabonds
as free slave labor or for other projects. The socioeconomic conditions
also provided additional incentives for the use of slave labor. Capitalist
ideology was not the decisive factor in these arrangements. One might
point to the Stalinist USSR where the massive use of slave labor was
routine and independent of any capitalist episteme. In dealing with vagabonds, the early modern state also exhibited other features. It combined
repressive policy with a peculiar sort of safety net where the prisons,
in a twisted way, became charitable institutions. This arrangement was
hardly specific to the rise of capitalism, for similar arrangements could
also be found in Stalinist USSR.

The Controversial Approach

The state and society were in general in accord in regard to vagabonds as dangerous misfits to be isolated and repressed. But society and the state machinery did not always work together. While both lower and upper classes saw vagabonds in general as a threat, there was sympathy among the populace for beggars, especially if they were children, old, and women. Moreover, not all vagabonds were dangerous criminals. Many did not congregate in large bands that could be perceived as an ultimate danger. There were many cases when vagabonds were limited, small groups, sometimes a family with women and children. They were harmless and pitiful creatures who inspired not fear but compassion among the peasants, and appreciation of harmless vagrants could occasionally be seen among peasants for various reasons.

Positive approaches to vagrants and similar folk were partially due to human nature, compassion for other human beings, if these humans were not a threat. Historically, poor wanderers without any property who were viewed as having no place in the social structure lived in another dimension, and people of this sort were spiritualized in the minds of the people. Their disinterest in the material world led them to be philosophers and religious or quasi-religious teachers, functions that were not separate in the minds of ancient people. With the spread of Christianity in the Middle Ages, vagrants who had been incorporated into various religious orders were often viewed as holy people. Helping them was a way to ensure entrance into paradise after death. This feeling was preserved in one sense or another during the early modern era. There was another sort of semi-mystical feeling that undoubtedly emerged in the minds of some peasants, even if they did not acknowledge it. The image of destitute people on the brink of starvation was quite depressing, and peasants quite vulnerable to a similar fate. Seeing vagabonds reminded people that, in the future, fate could play a brutal joke on them by crop failure or an over-zealous tax collector, and they could wind up in the same position. There was a subconscious contract with the deity that if they were kind to beggars, then someone might be kind to them in case of disaster.

All this led to a sporadic sense of social solidarity. "Indeed, at times a sense of common humanity and of resentment toward authority caused the small peasant to feel a closer bond with the vagrant than with the state officials, who were often seen as rapacious oppressors rather than protectors."[1] These considerations caused the peasants to help vagrants, if they were sure that they were harmless. "A kind of informal system of charity operated in much of rural France; peasants shared whatever little they had with vagrants and gave them shelter in a corner of the barn."[2] In most cases, however, peasants had not pity, but fear, especially of sturdy male vagabonds. The peasants' apprehension grew if they confronted gangs of male vagabonds. At that point the peasants supported the harshest treatment and were in absolute support of the state. Support of the state's harsh treatment of vagabonds of course did not exclude the opposite feeling—that the state was an oppressive force that extracted taxes from the people and supported the privileges of the elite. Still, the state's drive to maintain order by persecuting the vagabonds was appreciated, and in the state's harsh treatment of them in many ways followed not only its own interest and understanding of the reality but also the call of rudimentary public opinion.

Repression against Vagabonds

Throughout the sixteenth and seventeenth centuries, laws became increasingly harsh in dealing with vagabonds all over Western Europe. These people were arrested in mass preventive raids with a thoroughness that could rival any totalitarian state. This type of arrest increased sharply throughout the sixteenth century, especially in England. "In late sixteenth-century England only hundreds of vagrants were to be found in the search in the aftermath of Rising in the North (1571/2), while sixty years later reports to the Privy Council recorded the local arrest and punishment of many thousands of wandering rogues and sturdy beggars (nearly 25,000 in thirty-two English countries between 1631 and 1639)."[3] The numbers arrested tended to increase throughout the seventeenth century, not only in England "but also in the other European countries."

The situation was essentially the same in France, where "legislation on vagabondage had been revised in the direction of greater severity on several occasions since the seventeenth century."[4] More severe methods of punishment went along with increasing machinery of surveillance and "a tighter, more meticulous implementation of the law tended to take account of a mass of minor offenses that it once allowed to escape more easily."

Upon apprehension, marginals and out-and-out criminals whose offense did not warrant physical punishment or death could face different fates: relocation or deportation, usually to a distant colony, or imprisonment, where hospitals and prisons became the same institution.

Relocation/Deportation of Vagabonds

Relocation of marginal elements into certain areas of the cities was one popular way of dealing with the problem. This was an attempt to separate marginals permanently from the rest of the population. As Jütte noted, the emphasis was on "rigorous maintenance of a substantial distance from the marginal groups" (168). Special areas of separation of socially and medically dangerous elements started to emerge in various European cities. "In Medina del Campo and Segovia beggars were concentrated in peripheral areas as in Toledo, while in some other Spanish towns the pattern was distinct. When at the end of the fifteenth century more and more beggars settled in the town center the Frankfurt magistrates decreed that the beggars should no longer be permitted to dwell in the area called Liebfrauenberg but should be moved to Gilergrasse (beggars' lane)" (166).

The idea of relocation thus was connected to the spatial division of the city, a principle seen in many cities of the modern West. The assumption is that the segregated ghetto with its marginals would reduce the pressure on the rest of the population. Still, in these arrangements the marginals and the rest of the population shared common space, residency in the same city. Deportation implied complete separation of marginals from the rest of the population. Both ways of removing marginal groups were increasingly popular. In the future, deportation of the unreliable, potentially criminal people from the capital and other important cities of the realm would come into vogue among authoritarian and totalitarian governments. The practice of deporting undesirable people from the capital would be widely employed by the Tsarist and especially the Soviet regime.

The idea of deportation was not originally connected to the colonies. It had no implication of social engineering; it was not always intended to make beggars and other marginal elements useful members of society. The idea was originally quite simple: dangerous people should just leave the locality. Often, the intention was not even that they should leave the country, but just go to another place. Eventually, authorities started to prioritize the localities used. While they realized that they would not be able to clean the kingdom completely of all marginal elements, they could at least relieve the most political and socially sensitive places of their presence. These were usually the capitals and the locations of the courts.

In France, because of the emergence of the country's political culture, the emerging centralized bureaucracy, Paris as the capital started to play the role of head of the political the realm, and any malfunction of this head could lead to major political crises. This was a major reason why the French monarchy paid such attention to maintaining stability in the city. Not only out-and-out criminals were of concern, but any other asocial groups that disturbed public tranquility and that could also serve as a pool for criminals. Beggars were among these groups.

The state, the representatives of the central power as well as local self-government, joined their efforts to eradicate beggars. There were several ways of dealing with beggars; one was deportation. In other cases, beggars, as well as other marginal elements, were expelled from the locality, in this case from Paris. The king's desire to see Paris freed of vagabonds could be seen from the thirteenth century onward, when vagabonds began to be regarded not only as unfortunate people but also as a threat. In 1254 Louis IX published an edict against "idle people" called Les Establissements de Saint Louis stipulating "that people without steady incomes who led an 'evil life,' be expelled from the town."[5] In the fourteenth century Jean II Le Bon of France issued a similar edict.[6] As time progressed, the attitudes toward vagabonds became more and more harsh. One reason for this change in attitude was the increasing inability of society to accommodate the rising number of vagabonds. By 1400, hospitals in France were in crisis and increasingly unable to accommodate the beggars.[7] Repression and deportation were logically a better way of dealing with vagabonds than accommodation, and stress on repression increased even more by the sixteenth century. Beggars were especially intolerable in the capital; "on March 23, 1534, the order was given 'to poor scholars and indigents' to leave the city, and it was forbidden 'henceforth to sing hymns before images in the streets.'"[8] In some cases vagabonds were compelled to work, implicitly as justification for staying in particular localities; in other cases they were expelled.[9] Authorities were not concerned with where these people would eventually go. It could be just a nearby city.

As time progressed and the state became increasingly concerned with the totality of order, the notion grew that the entire realm should be free from crime and other elements that could be dangerous to society. Beggars were among these. But deportation of beggars from one part of the realm to another was not viewed as a wise solution. Removal of marginals from the capital to the provincial cities could hardly excite either residents or local officials in small villages where pressured vagabonds might move after being expelled from the capital and other key cities. The consensus became more and more clear that they should be removed from the realm completely. The growing power of the centralized state also meant it had the means to collect beggars and other similar folk all over the state and eject them from the territory. But unless they could be used as slave labor, other countries in Europe were equally anxious to relieve themselves of beggars. At this point deportation to a colony was invented as a desirable solution.

By the sixteenth and seventeenth centuries, several European powers had colonial possessions of various sizes. These colonies became an attractive place to send undesirable elements. However, deportation to a colony was possible only for powers with substantial colonial domains. The deported were to provide labor (they could actually fall into the condition of slavery) and populate new areas with the assumption that in the future these areas would generate income for the crown. This aspect of socioeconomic engineering made the absolutist state in many ways a pattern for totalitarian regimes of the future.

In the nineteenth century, both European powers and Imperial Russia commonly used the practice of sending undesirables to a distant land. In most cases these arrangements were purely pragmatic and often a spontaneous reaction to problems. They were not well planned. The absolutist regimes of seventeenth- and eighteenth-century Europe were different in this respect. France, more than any other country, attempted social engineering through deportation. Beginning at the end of the seventeenth century, the "royal government urged judges to impose penalty of transportation on men and women convicted of begging and vagrancy" (168). On some occasions, the courts deported up to six hundred of these creatures to populate the French colonies in America. The French did not act alone, for the British did the same. Children locked in houses of correction were deported, despite the children's revolts. Authorities continued to send "convicts to American colonies and later to Australia." This relocation was compulsory, voluntary, or semi-voluntary.

Moreover, shifting the unemployed to the emerging colonial empire was done on a rather grand scale. "Between 1660 and 1700 alone at least 100,000 persons emigrated from England to America" (190). Yet, due to rapid growth of population, emigration was not able to dispose of the excessive number of humans. Transatlantic migration was dangerous, and life in the new colonies was hard. Besides, countries with colonies were a minority, and those without colonies had no easy solution to over-population or increased crime. Thus deportation to the colonies was increasingly combined with securing of vagabonds and similar folk in workhouses. These establishments, with their brutal treatment of the inmates, could well compete with any Gulag-style institution.

The Use of Vagabonds

Besides deporting vagabonds another way of making them harmless to the rest of the society was to compel them to work. Historians have seen a different reason for spreading the idea of hard labor in the context of confinement. Most historians have related this phenomenon to the spread of capitalism and the introduction of what was called the "Protestant ethic." Max Weber emphasized that the creative part of the Protestant ethic, without which capitalism could not flourish, was pushing people into productive work and thereby restricting behavior. Foucault saw in the Protestant ethic the ideology that implicitly related production to increased control and then hard labor. Implicitly, in Foucault's view, the Protestant ethic paved the way for the reinstitution of slavery, and workhouse inmates were the prime victims of the new arrangements. This view became popular. "Everywhere in early modern Europe we find a new emphasis on the obligation to work. Labor became the new medicine for poverty.... The result of this changed perception of the able-bodied poor, labor in the eyes of poor relief reformers meant punishment of the idle as well as training and education" (199). While this reasoning in regard to the spread of the workhouses had its point, it could not explain everything, for the same principles led to the use of compulsory labor. Actual slave labor could be found in the Soviet USSR, as well as in other societies such as oriental despotism, none of which professed a "Protestant ethic." Thus, other explanatory models need to be tested to explain the rise of compulsory labor. Indeed, while slave labor had various causes, the rise of the power of the state was the most important. The state had acquired power, in many ways due to the rise of the state as the force that maintained security against internal and external enemies, and at the same time there was a pool of free labor available for exploitation. And the state here was easily tempted to use this pool of slave laborers for various projects.

Workhouses as Institutions of Punishment

While vagabonds were often deported to distant colonies or severely beaten, it was not this that gave rise to the indignation of those who studied the position of marginal people in early modern Europe but, rather, another type of punishment, the workhouses. "Compared to stigmatizing corporal punishment and other traditional measures of the social control such as expulsion and transportation, a new reformative policy of punishment in the form of so-called 'proto-penal institution' offered the authorities a kind of control over the offender without abusing his body" (169). The nature of these institutions and their social meaning was the point of much interpretation. Yet one role was central. Like other institutions that emerged at the dawn of the modern era, workhouses played an important role in repressive policies. They helped cleanse European society of asocial elements, reducing the pressure of asocial groups on the rest of society and ensuring a modicum of tranquility and basic public order. At the same time, workhouses became a useful economic institution that could achieve self-sufficiency and possibly even profit. Slave labor was integrated into the rising and increasingly efficient slave economy of the modern era. Workhouses also had other important functions. They created a web of protection, a safety net for those who fell out of the social structure. Of course, this was quite a twisted way of creating a safety net, at least from a present-day point of view.

State and societal repressiveness were deeply related to the rise of both marginal elements that bred crime and concern with personal safety. This was a major reason for the emergence of "workhouses." These institutions became a particular type of prison that separated dangerous groups from society. While the workhouse provided a pool of free labor and served as a repressive institution, it is clear that the repressive aspect of the workhouse was more important than economics. Indeed, at the beginning of this process the workhouses were more organs of repression than a reservoir of cheap labor. They actually institutionalized hard labor in the form of slavery, as a primarily punitive arrangement.

The attempt to care for the poor in church-sponsored or similar types of institutions where the repressive/controlling aspect was as important as charity had a long history in Europe in general and in France in particular. Society's attempts to care for the poor and displaced in an institutionalized way went back to the Dark Ages in the sixth century,[10] and in the ninth century the Hôtel-Dieu, one of the first church-supported hospitals, was created.[11] Even in the early periods of their existence the hospitals were not so much charitable institutions as prisons, a fusion of punishment and charity. Jules Michelet stated, "The old hospitals were in no way different from houses of correction. The sick, the poor, the prisoners who were thrown into them were always seen as sinners struck down by God, who first had to expiate their sins. They suffered cruel treatment. So terrible a charity appalled people."[12] Geremek admitted that this vision of hospitals was "too gloomy," at least for the earlier periods. But the repressive nature of the confinement increased as time progressed and views toward vagabonds became more and more harsh.

The use of the church/monastery as a place of confinement, the rising use of slavery and semi-slavery both in Europe and in the newly discovered colonies, paralleled with the increasing power of the states, were all major motivations for the creation of these new institutions of isolation and punishment of marginals of all types. As a result, the workhouses and refuges for vagabonds, with often strict discipline and appalling conditions, started to proliferate all over Europe. In some cases these workhouses developed into big enterprises. Some institutions took care of three hundred inmates.

Britain was apparently among the first nations to launch this enterprise. This was not surprising because England belonged to the European countries where the laws on vagabonds were greatly elaborated and most stringent, at least in comparison with France.[13] Jütte noted, "In 1553 Edward VI, influenced by Bishop Nicolas Ridley, conveyed an old, decayed palace, the Bridewell, to the city of London, for the safekeeping, punishing and setting to work of idle poor and vagabonds. Other English towns (e.g., Norwich, Ipswich) followed in 1560" (169). The arrangements were institutionalized and the "Poor Relief Act of 1576 ordered the establishment of so-called 'houses of correction in all countries and corporate towns of the realm.'" The act "prescribed the construction of houses of correction, to number at least one per county. Their upkeep was to be assured by tax, but the public was encouraged to make voluntary donations."[14]

The arrangement was that at first the person was not just separated from the rest of society but compelled to work. Officially, this was done for the purpose of reforming the individual. In reality, it was an introduction to hard labor and virtual slavery, and this punishment through work was one of the major goals. Originating in England, the institutions soon spread all over Europe. In some cases, these were not direct copies of the English model, but emerged independently.

Italians apparently introduced similar institutions independent of English influence. The Italian institutions were more humanitarian and apparently did not push the inmates to work. Indeed, one of the first establishments of this sort emerged when Pope "Sixtus V established the famous beggar's hospital of Ponte Sisto in Rome in 1587. Similar hospitals were founded in Turin (1583) and Moderna (1592)" (173). Germany was also active in institutionalizing these workhouses. "In German-speaking countries, it was marked by the creation of houses of correction, the Zuchthausern; the first antedates the French houses of confinement (except for the Charité of Lyons); it opened in Hamburg around 1620."[15] Institutions of this type soon spread all over Germany and "were founded in the second half of the century: Basel (1667), Breslau (1668), Frankfort (1684), Spandau (1684), Konigsberg (1691)."

With the above exception, the idea to use inmates as free labor was in the minds of organizers of the workhouses from the beginning of the enterprise. This idea was deeply connected to the idea of semi-slave labor that could be seen since the late Middle Ages. This emphasis on the economic productivity of inmate labor proliferated with the advancement of time, especially in the seventeenth century.

Workhouses as Economic Institutions

The emphasis on work became crucially important to Foucault and his followers, who elaborated on how the system of control emerged in Western capitalist society. They implied that one way of achieving control was to force everyone to work. The work ethic implied that each person should be attached to some institution, factory, school, or barracks. If for any reason one found himself outside these institutions, he should be incorporated into a workhouse. In this "Grand Panopticon" into which modern capitalist society was transformed, the workhouse had an important place and was especially disliked.

Foucault connected the emphasis on work and workhouses to the general spread of the Weberian type of work ethic. The "episteme" of emerging capitalism took hold of the elite, in fact of society in general, and compelled the authorities to push the inmates to work. As in his explanation of torturous deaths of the criminals on the scaffold, Foucault suggested that the reasons for compelling the authorities to push the inmates to work were purely ideological. The cult of work was related to the spirit and ideology of the capitalist society. This assumption must be questioned, however.

To start with, the idea that work was the road to moral regeneration was hardly related to capitalism. St. Paul, in the New Testament, proclaimed that those who did not work should not eat. This statement was incorporated into the "moral codex of the builder of the Communism" in the USSR, whose ideology professed absolute opposition to capitalism. Foucault stated that the workhouses were intimately related to the capitalist factories, army, and other regimented institutions of the emerging capitalist society. This was true, but the workhouses and the use of semi-slave labor in this or that institutional setting could be related to the

Stalinist GULAG as well as to oriental despots.[16] As a matter of fact it was this type of society that used slave labor in truly grand proportions. At the same time, semi-slave labor, including institutional use, was an essential part of pre-modern European history. The major reason for slave labor was not ideology, but pragmatism and certain societal conditions. The large numbers of marginals, the existence of the state machinery to compel them to work, and the general profitability of slave labor led to an attempt to establish workhouses as a place of incarceration and profitable enterprise. However, pragmatic considerations did not preclude ideological moralizing as justification for these arrangements. It was asserted that work and confinement would reeducate the person, help to integrate him eventually into straight society, and save his soul.

The idea of work as punishment and reeducation was not just rooted in the first experiments with compulsory, slave labor in open spaces, but also had other historical roots. It was an institution with precedents in the church in general and the monastery in particular. In many ways the workhouses emerged from church institutions whose origins could be traced over centuries. The medieval church could be regarded as the first institution that provided a safety net as well as removing undesirable and marginal people from society. The cloisters and churches provided people with safety net arrangements, but put them at the absolute mercy of the institution to live according to strict rules that divided the day between work and prayer. From the institution of the medieval church emerged hospitals.

By the sixteenth and seventeenth centuries, the church-supported system that provided a network of protection for the most destitute members of society grew, accompanied by a much more stringent system of control and repressiveness. Places of refuge for the destitute became indistinguishable from prisons, for work was seen as being as important as prayers. The nature of confinement had changed. In the public mind, confinement became coupled to the idea of labor. The introduction of hard labor into confinement made inmates into virtual slaves.

At the beginning there were assumptions that marginal elements could be compelled to work and consequently be punished and reeducated in open spaces. They could be segregated from cities and chained or guarded. The local government arranged a sort of local hard labor. The assumption was that these institutions should not just punish or isolate vagabonds and provide conditions for their moral or social regeneration but also be profitable and useful.

A 1350 ordinance against vagabonds implied that they should have gainful employment.[17] A 1371 ordinance proclaimed that those without work must be available for public work in Paris. In 1367, a royal proclamation stated that those without work must "present themselves at the sites where the town ditches were being repaired."[18] And those who persisted with their idleness must be punished. Similar ordinances were made in 1388, 1389, and 1413.[19]

On 23 December 1486, the Parlement made another edict against vagabonds,[20] and in 1523 there was a royal edict against vagabonds.[21] "In 1532, the Parliament of Paris decided to arrest beggars and force them to work in the sewers of the city, chained in pairs."[22] In 1533, the Estates of Languedoc were upset by the activities of vagabonds and "the notables petitioned the King for the legislation against the 'multitude' of poor who continued to disrupt municipal life. François I responded in 1534 with a decree ordering sturdy beggars to be put to work on public works projects; the infirm, women with children were to be supported by their respective parishes."[23]

The idea of using sturdy beggars for public works, essentially for hard labor, was spreading in the provinces. It was not as much the king's ordinance as local initiatives that led to mass use of the beggars as slave labor. In Toulouse, there was anxiety about "public order, morality and health" and crime.[24] These problems stimulated the cleansing of the city of vagabonds and similar asocial elements. The apprehension of the vagabonds had another rationale as well. "Beginning in the 1530s municipal officials began to pursue an aggressive, if ad hoc, policy of urbanization, from road repair and bridge construction to the renovation of municipal building." The essentially slave labor of the vagabonds was quite profitable and widely used. The combination of these two types of incentive led to police raids and sending vagabonds to work often "in collars and chains."[25] The same practice could be found in sixteenth-century Paris where "incorrigible vagrants" toil "in chains under guard to the city's fortifications."[26] Parisian vagabonds were also physically punished.[27] By the middle of the sixteenth century, the authorities had decided to organize a specialized institution to take care of the vagabonds, and the Grand Bureau des Pauvres was established in Paris in 1554.[28] On the surface, this Bureau's major role was charitable, to help the poor. But it was also engaged in repressive functions, and was concerned with the socially acceptable use of the poor, an idea that started to circulate in the sixteenth century.[29] In these conditions, the idea of a "Hospital General was in the air."[30]

The Hôpital Général that emerged in the seventeenth century would try to use places of confinement as both a place of repression and control and an economically viable organization. While it is one of the most famous of all seventeenth-century institutions, mostly due to Foucault's work, it was not the only one. Similar institutions proliferated all over Europe. In the majority of these institutions punishment and isolation were connected to semi-slave labor.

Italian institutions were rather humanitarian and inspired by desire to help the unfortunate, but other institutions of this type were concerned not with marginals but with society. Their goal was to separate marginal elements from society and keep them locked up with minimal expense. There was even the assumption, at least at the beginning, that these houses of correction should generate profit. For this reason, the workhouses in most countries were actually prisons and hard labor institutions converged into one. In many cases, they remained a Gulag-type of establishment. Indeed, Jütte said, "most English houses of correction maintained a strict discipline. Admission was accompanied by whipping, followed by incarceration and hard labor. The day was regimented. The inmates of Norwich house of correction, for example, were supposed to work from 5 A.M. to 8 P.M. in summer, with half an hour to eat and fifteen minutes to pray" (170). Inmates who refused to work were severely beaten and their meager food allowances cut even more.

Similar prisons emerged in Holland, directly inspired by the English. The Dutch humanist "Dirck Volckertsz Coornhert launched the idea that the idle poor be disciplined by hard work and that in every town a gaol-like institution should be erected for the punishment of sturdy beggars, rogues and deviants" (170-71). Created in Amsterdam, it was called the *tuchthuis*, where the inmates engaged in rasping wood. "In the Netherlands, confinement of beggars and criminals became a regular practice during the seventeenth century. About twenty-six Dutch towns imitated the example of Amsterdam, by establishing similar institutions for the employment of the idle poor and the correction of offenders" (171).

The Amsterdam workhouses became famous mostly because of the prominence the establishment received in Foucault's work. "The foundation of the Amsterdam tuchthuis was a landmark in the history of a vast program of social engineering, known since Michel Foucault's work in this field as 'the Great Confinement.'"[31] The interest Foucault brought to the Amsterdam arrangements was due to his political philosophy that saw Western capitalism as brutally oppressive and in need of Gulag-type arrangements in the paradigm of a capitalist work ethic.

Slave labor was also used for military purposes. Slaves as soldiers was quite an ancient tradition. The case of Mameluke slave soldiers is well known. Yet as a soldier the Mameluke slave lost or at least changed his original position and ruled Egypt and Syria from 1250 to 1517. In the early modern era slaves as military personnel were used as rowers in the fleet. Punishment by sending to the galleys was widespread in early modern Europe.[32] This was a departure from the practice of antiquity where the rowers were poor but free citizens, as in ancient Greece.[33]

In France punishment by sending to the galleys was introduced at the end of the fifteenth century. "In 1496, Charles VIII finally gave the order to send the unemployed and the vagabonds to the galleys. The desire to eliminate the social peril went hand in hand with the attempt to make the useless useful."[34] In 1516 this sort of punishment was institutionalized and confirmed by a new royal edict.[35] In fact, one could state that execution by the wheel and the galley were the major innovations in the system of punishment brought about by the sixteenth century.[36] As a result of this edict, in a few years the numbers of those sent to the galleys had risen by a factor of at least twenty to fifty.[37] The quick proliferation of sending to the galley as a punishment even led to the decline of numbers of people condemned to capital punishment.[38]

The Profitability of Slavery

The use of semi-slave labor cannot be interpreted exclusively in the context of the episteme paradigm. This explanation implied that people were pushed to work because of ideological considerations. Either the "Protestant ethic" of emerging capitalism or the ethic of socialist society pushed the rulers to use semi-slave labor. According to this interpretation, the ideological and punishing nature of the institutions, not the goal of profit, was the reason for this labor. This assumption, however, can be questioned. It is true that not all these economic arrangements were profitable, and a desire to isolate and punish vagabonds pushed the elite to employ this sort of punishment. Yet one could assume that semi-slave labor was not just an important byproduct of the punitive system, but also a profitable undertaking, and in many cases the profitability of slave labor was one of the major reasons for its use. This explains the spread of this type of labor in the beginning of the modern era and its return in the twentieth century.

The relationship between employers and employees has changed vastly over the course of history. Historians could challenge the assumption that practices of personal dependence were only a feature of pre-modern society where the lower classes were personally dependent on their masters. Contractual free labor emerged in the capitalist era. But this practice was drastically reversed over the course of the twentieth century. Most totalitarian regimes actively employed slave labor. Sending people to concentration camps, modern dictators, like rulers of the early modern era, were concerned with isolating and eliminating real or imagined troublemakers wherever they could be found.

Economic considerations were also on their minds, and in some cases were the major considerations for sending people to the camps. This was the case with the Stalinist regime, which used slave labor for a variety of projects in the crash industrialization program. Quite a few Western historians, of course, would challenge the assumption that the rapid industrialization that changed backward Russia into an industrial giant was hardly the product of enthusiastic workers exemplified by Stakhanov, the coal miner who exhibited unusual feats of productivity. The transformation was due to the slave-type work of millions of Gulag inmates.

A variety of intellectuals, especially after the works of Alexander Solzhenitsyn, the seminal Russian writer and historian, have elaborated on the role of the concentration camps with millions of inmates as the socioeconomic foundation of the Stalinist regime. In the view of these observers, slave labor was a manifestation of the totalitarian nature of the regime. This regime was seen as an aberration of history. It was "abnormal" in its essence, and the absence of private property and market was one manifestation of this abnormality. Slave labor was directly connected to the economic and political features of the Soviet system and implicitly connected to the economic problems of the USSR. Yet, both in the Stalinist USSR and in the modern West, slave labor was quite often profitable. The great leap in the proliferation of slavery began when capitalism started to take hold in the West. This spread of slavery was often free from any intention of controlling and punishing. The intentions were plainly economic. Slaves and the slave trade were a profitable enterprise.[39] The efficiency and proliferation of slave labor could be seen in various parts of the globe that responded to capitalism with its emphasis on efficiency and profit.

To start with, slavery proliferated in America where the plantations required a large number of workers. The local population could not always be used and in many cases its number dwindled. As a result, mass importation of slaves from Africa began in the sixteenth century and over the course of centuries millions of them were brought to America. They were transported and often exploited in a way hardly different from that of inmates in the Gulag, especially when supplies were plentiful and costs comparatively low. The spread of slavery in the form of serfdom was also seen in Europe, mostly in Eastern Europe. The so-called "New Edition of Serfdom" reversed the trend for decreasing personal dependence. In many ways the position of the serfs was not much different from that of slaves. In Russia, the sixteenth and seventeenth centuries witnessed a steady limitation on the rights of peasants to move from one landlord to another, and peasants were finally fixed to the land by 1649.

In all these arrangements, ideology was hardly the guiding principle. Neither American planters nor Russian landlords were concerned with the purifying role of labor or the punitive implications of slavery. They only considered their economic interests. One could hardly assume that they employed Gulag-type labor only because they were deceived by ideological paradigms. Slavery was profitable and therefore efficient.

The profitability of semi-slave labor had not escaped the mind of state authorities. In Western Europe the situation had peculiarities. Personal slavery and serfdom were mostly gone. However, its profitability was well remembered. Thus, there was an additional impetus for building workhouses. They were often a way of receiving slave labor, especially when free labor was expensive. Indeed, "Outside of the periods of crisis, confinement acquired another meaning. Its repressive function was combined with a new use. It was no longer merely a question of confining those out of work, but of giving work to those who had been confined and thus making them contribute to the prosperity of all. The alternative is clear: cheap manpower in the periods of full employment and high salaries; and in periods of unemployment, re-absorption of the idle and social protection against agitation and uprisings."[40]

The Problems of the Security Net: From the Pre-Modern to the Modern Era

Not all people engaged in asocial behavior were representatives of the lower classes whose involvement in crime was the direct result of their misery. Yet in many cases this was precisely true. It was clear that the state and society saw repression and control as a way of dealing with criminals, or those groups of the population who could be seen as breeding crime and similar problems for society. However, both the state and society assumed that repression alone would not solve the problems. Repression would be combined with a safety net. This safety net became deeply interwoven with the repressive and controlling aspect of the new social and political and ideological arrangements. In order to understand these arrangements one needs to review how the safety net existed in the pre-modern era and how it started to change. The pre-modern safety net was related to a familial style of dependence, a patriarchal type of slavery. The new type of safety net, also related to dependence/slavery, in some cases was much harsher than the previous one.

It is wrong to assume that the safety net was a creation of modern capitalism. On the contrary, the safety net constituted the essence of pre-modern society. But it was designed differently from the safety net of modern capitalism. Society had been organized along familial, *Gemein-schaft* lines, where members were not only restrained in their behavior by the norm of the group, but also had an obligation to support their kin in case troubles. These ties of mutual obligation were, according to some historians, the essence of the feudal relationship. Maksim Kovalevskii, a well-known Russian scholar with a European reputation, was among the first who developed these notions about feudalism. He developed this idea in his book, *The Origin of Modern Democracy*, later hailed by critics as one of the masterpieces of sociological thought.[41]

Kovalevskii stated that the rule of feudal barons was not based exclusively on force, and that force played a rather minor role in the arrangements. The feudal lord and the peasantry engaged in a special contract. According to this unwritten agreement, the peasantry had to pay in cash and in kind, perform different services to the lord, and in some instances tolerate the most humiliating treatment, for example, the right of the "first night" where the feudal lord could claim the right to spend the first night with a newly married woman.[42] At the same time, the lord was obliged to protect the peasantry from foreign forces and provide them with food and other commodities in calamities. Even stronger was the obligation between members of a family. Tradition strongly required them to support each other. These obligations were especially strong for children toward their parents. Filial piety was a virtue in most ancient religions and traditional societies. In some, like Confucianism, it was a major virtue.

The assumption that close relatives took care of most people is an explanation for the fact that medieval hospitals were often quite selective in choosing whom they wished to help. In some cases, this practice extended to the early modern era. "Early modern hospitals did not provide in the first place care and medical assistance for the ill; rather they housed and cared for pilgrims, travelers, orphans, the aged and the destitute."[43] Yet as time progressed arrangements changed.

The dissolution of traditional society at the advent of the modern era eroded the traditional system of support. Many people had no place to go in the face of famine, sickness, and similar calamities. They had no safety net and limited employment opportunities, and those lucky enough to be employed could easily lose their jobs. Constant insecurity and ravages of pestilence made death one of the most important themes in the intellectual discourse of the early modern era. "Up to the second half of the fifteenth century, or even a little beyond, the theme of death reigns alone. The end of man, the end of time, bear the face of pestilence and war. What overhangs human existence is this conclusion and this order from which nothing escapes. The presence that threatens even within this world is a flesh less one."[44]

To be sure, marginals were seen as a threat, especially if there were many. Repression or isolation and the desire to generate profits were the major thrusts of society's policy. Yet these were not separated from the notions of protection and responsibility. Dealing with these people followed a different pattern. In some cases the emphasis was only on charitable activity. In these situations society regarded the beggar as unable to earn his daily bread. It apparently decided to provide legitimization for groups of beggars and started to license them in a way.

This process of legitimization of beggars was complicated by the problem of dividing them into those who deserved public assistance and those who did not. The former were people who were not able to support themselves, the latter were only lazy. The beginning of this division could be seen by the twelfth century.[45] It became quite clear by the late Middle Ages when, in some cases, "municipal authorities issued badges or tokens to show that the beggars wearing them were begging with the approval of the authorities, as was still the case in seventeenth-century Scotland, "where the Kirk made such signs or begging licenses compulsory." Later on, when begging had become prohibited, the same sign served as a distinctive mark for those who were on the dole."[46]

Several French royal decrees (1572 and 1580) emphasized the need for the church to be actively engaged in charity toward vagabonds, especially in time of famine and plague.[47] There was nothing new in this appeal, for the church had been one of the major institutions that cared for the poor and other marginal elements of society since the Middle Ages.[48] Besides the church, various municipal bodies were engaged in the charitable activities. In Paris, for example, "municipal institutions of poor relief had their beginnings in 1505."[49] The idea that the poor and marginals must be taken care of and separated from the general public could be found by the end of the sixteenth century in the mind of the local elite.[50] By the middle of the sixteenth century there was an expansion of the charitable activities of the local hospitals.[51]

While the charitable activity of private individuals, churches, and similar institutions was helpful, it did not solve the problems of many poor people, especially in periods of famine and disease. During calamities, a great many people had no place to go. In this situation, the workhouses in various forms were the only institutions that could help them. By taking in and absorbing these people, the workhouses revealed a peculiar role that the prison system started to play in early modern society. While prisons were indeed repressive institutions, places that could generate income, they were also a shelter and safe place where people could receive at least some nourishment. This idea of providing a basic security net for the increasing numbers of marginal people was behind the creation of the workhouses and similar institutions all over Europe, beside the other considerations—punishment, isolation, and cheap slave labor.

Humanitarian considerations, of course, were not a major driving force in creating the workhouses. But it is clear that these considerations were in the minds of those who designed these penal institutions. Support now came from the society as a whole. Either civic society, which started to emerge especially in countries such as Holland, or the state confronted the increasing numbers of asocial elements. For this reason, the workhouses both increased the means of repressiveness and developed the idea of a safety net on a broad scale. The system of a safety net was especially important in a society that had undergone the end of the traditional structure, where members of society were both controlled and protected by such institutions as the peasant commune, the guilds, and the broad family network. These structures of traditional societies were replaced by institutions that would protect the destitute regardless of their clan or group origins. Here, the role of the workhouses is not to be underestimated. They were one of the first attempts to create a system of social support outside the familial circle and the church, which had been the only institution of support outside the family network in pre-modern society.

It was clear that the workhouses as they emerged were brutal institutions. They were forms of slave labor with malnutrition and routine beatings. Their major goal in their first centuries was not to provide shelter and food but to remove dangerous individuals from society and to be self-sufficient or even generate income. It was also clear that the spirit of capitalism influenced the idea that one should work and be productive. But these pragmatic considerations were not the only goal. The workhouses, with their slave style arrangements, provided a twisted form of safety net.

The assumption that security is tantamount to slavery was firmly placed in the context of the *Gemeinschaft* society that preceded the capitalist era. The residual aspects of pre-modern familial relationships survived for a long time even in Western societies. The chief of the household needed to provide for the members of his family (children), and members of this family, children first of all, were at the absolute disposal of the father of the family. He had the right to beat them, sell them into slavery, or even kill them. This idea goes back centuries and has roots in ancient Jewish law (for example, the sacrifice of Isaac by Abraham), traditional Chinese law, and Roman law. In Roman law, the father had more power over his children than over his slaves. Slaves, once free, could not be taken back into slavery. But if a son whose father sold him into slavery became free, he returned to his father. Only after several rounds of enslavement and liberation could the father lose his power over his son

This arrangement, where social relationships were patterned after family relationships, could be seen in the Roman tradition of patron and clients. The same arrangements were an essential aspect of the life in the Middle Ages where the feudal lord took the role of the quasi-father in his relationship to the peasants, who in this case became his children. This role might be one explanation of the "surprisingly high status of those who voluntarily became 'serfs.'"[52] The arrangements of the pre-modern era were reinforced in the workhouses by the new spirit of capitalism, which emphasized utility in the possession of slaves and other persons under one's command. The same spirit implied that work not only generated profit but was important for a person's moral uplifting, for the reeducation of the morally guilty. It also implied a sort of twisted protection against the vagaries of life.

These arrangements were quite similar not only to pre-modern society but also to the modern totalitarian regime. Indeed, in the Soviet system, both Gulag style slave labor and the ease with which the state could dispose of citizens by means of slave camps were inseparable from the assumption that the state should guarantee a minimum of food and shelter for the majority.

The critics of the workhouse see problems with the brutal slavery that provided morsels of food and dubious shelters for slave work as a safety net. But for early modern Europe there were no other realistic alternatives beside extermination or deportation for dealing with the hordes of marginals who emerged in Europe as the old social structures collapsed.

At the same time, one could state that the implied alternative could be reduced to the simple principle of leaving these people alone. Many of those on the Left who observed early modern vagrants and tramps have related to the image of hippies indirectly connected to the entire philosophy of the Left in the 1960s. Leftist philosophy related the hippie phenomenon to a spontaneous unmolested life, a Rousseau style Utopia where there were neither legalistic restraints nor a definite norm, and where order emerged in a spontaneous way because humans are naturally good. There was also the implicit assumption that society would somehow provide minimal necessities and the police, of course, would provide basic security. Yet, the marginals of the early modern era did not live in hippie conditions. Food and other necessities were precious commodities. It is not surprising, then, that the image of health was related not to thinness (as is the case with the modern West) but rather to corpulence and even obesity. As François Rabelais imagined it, the utopian paradise was a place of gluttony.

There was neither food nor easily available shelter. Disease was rampant, and the climate of most of Europe was not similar to California. So if they pursued a peaceful existence and did not engage in attacks on people, most vagabonds would die. One could argue that, despite all the vagaries of free living, vagabonds would rather live and die as free individuals than be placed in prison-type establishments. However, society undoubtedly would have suffered from the freedom of vagabonds, who would in most cases become criminals and impact society negatively.

Economic Regulation as a Charitable Activity

Charity was a byproduct of the repressive machinery when it dealt with large numbers of marginals. The major goal of the state was to remove this potentially dangerous group from society and, if possible, to use them as a source of cheap labor. The charitable aspect was marginal. Still, it existed and was integrated into the growing power of the state, which became increasingly intrusive in the life of the society, regulating such intimate aspects of life as the sexual relationship in general and marriage in particular. This broad involvement in the political, economic, social, and private lives of citizens caused the state to develop totalitarian aspects. One obvious aspect was the ruthless use of all resources for rapid economic advancement. Surplus human material was broadly used as semi-slave labor. The repressive side of this treatment of the populace as a reservoir of labor was tightly integrated into other aspects of the totalitarian rule, along with the idea of social protection in its various forms.[53] The aspect of social protection could be seen even in the early projects of the workhouses. Despite the prison-like conditions in these institutions, the chance for survival there was greater than outside houses, especially during famine.

This aspect of the workhouse was integrated into the broad social and economic design of the early modern state. It was implied that the duty of the ruler was not only to protect subjects from asocial processes and related calamities (crime, invasion, spread of pandemic disease), but also to guarantee basic subsistence. Thus, the regulation of prices became an essential duty of the early modern kings.

The high price of basic commodities led to frequent food riots where the populace usually attacked the merchants, accusing them of keeping prices too high. The crowd saw the merchants as selfish profiteers whose interests excluded the lives and well-being of fellow humans. The crowds demanded "fair" prices that made it possible for simple folk to have food. This demand for cheaper food as a postulate of morality rather than of economic drives made possible for Edward P. Thompson to elaborate his well-known theory of "moral economy."[54]

The economic demands of the masses were important signals to the elite. Yet it was not the masses with their instinctive moral-cum-socialist thinking that organized price controls. This originated at the state level, in most cases only when the state had achieved totalitarian power. Indeed, Diocletian (284-305 A.D.) was among the first Western rulers to introduce price controls. Diocletian's reign was transitional in the sense that it signified the move from Principate, early empire, to Dominatus, when the Roman Empire became quite close to Oriental despotism. Diocletian acted in totalitarian fashion, as a divine ruler with unlimited power. In 301 A.D., he introduced his *Edictum de Maximis Pretiis*, which fixed wages and established maximum prices "to prevent inflation, abusive profits, and the exploitation of buyers. About 1,000 articles were enumerated, and violation was punishable by death; severe penalties were exacted of black marketers."[55] The French state returned to the practice of the regulation of the prices only after more than a thousand years, at a time when the state had mastered enough force for such an undertaking. Similar to Diocletian, oriental despots, and totalitarian rulers such as Stalin, the French kings assumed that they had a right to intervene in the lives of the subjects on a broad scale, but also the obligation to ensure the supply of basic goods. The Soviet ideologists would proudly announce that only its socialist regime thought about the economic well-being of the populace, and this was an essential difference from the bourgeois regimes of the West. Contrary to Soviet ideologists, neither Diocletian nor French kings elaborated their ideas about the importance of subsistence control in such a way. Still the framework of their minds was essentially the same.

Providing food was seen from the sixteenth century onward as an essential aspect of the king's obligations. "Though it was never inscribed in the fundamental laws of the realm, the commitment to subsistence became, in the vernacular, a responsibility and an attribute of kingship. It was not merely something the monarch-father did for his subject-children; it was something he was expected and in some sense required to do."[56] Jacques Bossuet, one of the leading ideologists of French absolutism in the sixteenth century, assumed that this was the case. "Doctrinaire of absolutism and divine monarchy, Jacques Bossuet asserted that the king's obligation to ensure subsistence was the 'foundation' of all his claims on his people."[57] This assumption stipulated regulation of prices for bread and other essential commodities. The idea that the market was to be regulated was also a cardinal idea for the local city government. The city authorities did not advocate the free fluctuation of prices on essential commodities, such as bread and rent.[58] During times of famine, they searched the houses of residents suspected of hoarding bread.[59]

Notes

1. Gordon Wright, *Between the Guillotine and Liberty: Two Centuries of the Crime Problem in France* (New York: Oxford University Press, 1983), 9.
2. Ibid., 8, 9.
3. Robert Jütte, *Poverty and Deviance in Early Modern Europe* (Cambridge: Cambridge University Press, 1994), 148 (citations in parentheses in text).
4. Foucault, *Discipline and Punish*, 76.
5. Geremek, *The Margins*, 30.
6. Schnapper, "La repression du vagabondage," 146.
7. Leslie Goldsmith, "Poor Relief and Reform in Sixteenth-Century Orléans" (Ph.D. dissertation, 1980), 65.
8. Foucault, *Madness and Civilization*, 47.
9. Goldsmith, *Poor Relief*, 238; Gonthier, *Le châtiment du crime*, 62; Laurent Coste, "Bordeaux et la peste dans la première moitié du XVIIe siècle," *Annales du Midi* 110, 224 (1998): 474.
10. Goldsmith, *Poor Relief*, 58.
11. Daniel Roche, "Paris capitale des pauvres: quelques reflexions sur le pauperisme parisien entre XVIIe et XVIIIe siècle," *Mélanges de l'Ecole française de Rome, Moyen Age, temps modernes* 99, 2 (1987): 843.
12. Geremek, *The Margins*, 169.
13. Schnapper, "La repression du vagabondage," 151.
14. Foucault, *Madness and Civilization*, 43.
15. Ibid.
16. It was not accidental that Karl Wittfogel (1896-1988) made the implicit comparison between the socialist regime and oriental despotism.
17. Gonthier, *Délinquance*, 149.
18. Geremek, *The Margins*, 34.

19. Ibid., 36-37.
20. Philippe Sassier, *Du bon usage des pauvres: histoire d'un thème politique (XVIe-XXe siècle)* (Paris: Fayard, 1990), 62.
21. Schnapper, "Justice criminelle," 279.
22. Foucault, *Madness and civilization*, 47.
23. Davis, "Poverty and Poor Relief" (dissertation), 448.
24. Davis, "Poverty and Poor Relief," *Historical Reflections*, 285.
25. Ibid.
26. Alexander Cowan, *Urban Europe 1500-1700* (London: Arnold, 1998), 160. On the push for vagabonds to work in Orléans, see also Goldsmith, *Poor Relief*, 35.
27. Babelon, *Paris*, 190.
28. Sassier, *Du bon usage*, 63.
29. Ibid., 109.
30. Dartiguenave, *Marginalité*, 44.
31. Ibid.
32. Langbein, *Torture*, 30.
33. Ernle Bradford, *The Battle for the West: Thermopylae* (New York: McGraw-Hill, 1980), 76.
34. Geremek, *The Margins,* 41.
35. Schnapper, "La repression du vagabondage," 150.
36. Soman, "Sorcellerie, justice criminelle et société," 201.
37. Schnapper, "Justice criminelle," 266, 267.
38. Ibid., 271, 274.
39. The economic profitability of slavery could be seen from the fact it was profitable in America until the end of slavery as an institution. The end of slavery was in no way connected to economics.
40. Foucault, *Madness and Civilization*, 51.
41. M. M. Kovalevskii, *Proiskhozhdenie sovremennoi demokratii*, 4 vols. (Moscow: A.I. Mamontova, 1895-1897).
42. Some modern historians question that this happened and regard it as an invention of historians.
43. Jütte, *Poverty*, 191.
44. Foucault, *Madness and Civilization*, 15.
45. Schnapper, "La repression du vagabondage," 144.
46. Jütte, *Poverty,* 160.
47. Marie-Claude Dinet-Lecomte, "Bureaux et maisons de charite: L'assistance à domicile aux 'pauvres malades' dans le cadre des paroisses toulousaines (1686-1797)," *Revue d'Histoire de l'Église de France* 80, 205 (1994): 217.
48. Gager, "Comme leur propre enfant," 149.
49. Loats, "Gender and Work," 15. On charitable institutions see also Gager, "Comme leur propre enfant," 151.
50. Daniel Hickey, "Closing Down Local Hospitals in Seventeenth-Century France: The Mount Carmel and St. Lazare Reform Movement," *Histoire Sociale—Social History* 25, 49 May 1992): 11.
51. Ibid., 21.
52. Michael Jones, "When Was Feudalism?" *Times Literary Supplement*, 6 March 1998, 26.
53. Historians who condemned the Soviet regime pointed to slave labor as the foundation of the Soviet economy; those who praised the system pointed to the protective aspects of the Soviet state. The two aspects were actually interwoven and could not exist without each other.

54. E. P. Thompson, "The Moral Economy of the English Crowd in the Eighteenth Century," *Past and Present* 50 (1971).
55. "Diocletian," *Encyclopedia Britannica Online*.
56. Steven Laurence Kaplan, "Provisioning Paris: The Crisis of 1738-1741," in Mc-Clain et al., *Edo and Paris*, 175.
57. Ibid.
58. Holt, "Order," 63.
59. Davis, *Poverty*, 245; On the search of the houses of the potential speculators in the Toulouse see also Davis, "Poverty," *Historical Reflections/Reflexions Historiques* 17: 275.

7

The Result of the Repression

As this work has stated, early modern Europe and France in particular experienced a revolution. This was not the revolution that would come later—the transition from one political and social order to another. Rather, a process of meltdown led to the proliferation of various asocial and antisocial processes, ranging from crime to exercising one's biological functions, whether lovemaking or defecation/urination. This asocial/antisocial behavior implied that these individuals were anomie in the sense that they were directed not against this or that group, but against society as a whole. These people were in many ways identical to the "anomies" that could be found in the modern West. Yet there was a substantial difference. In the modern West the anomie was relegated to the margins of society and the asocial process rarely if ever challenged the existence of the society. In early modern Europe (France is a notable example) the asocial process and asocial individuals threatened the existence of society. Those who were engaged in this asocial process were from not just the lower classes, as is often the case in the modern West, but all groups of society. Bandits, one of the most dangerous asocial groups in any society, included all classes, from nobles to peasants.

Thus, the emerging state was in a condition of continuous emergency and launched a "reign of terror" not as a result of the emergence of a new "episteme" or ideology, but because of the pressing needs of society. In other words, ideology played a secondary role. What was the result of this brutal application of punishment? While there was some improvement in security, the term taken here in its holistic meaning, in sixteenth-century France there was no clear reversal of the process and another century would be needed for the emergence of islands of comparative security amid the asocial behavior of various sorts.

There were signs of the benefits of repression and the security that emerged as a result of the rise of the absolutist state and the proliferation of the repressive/protective policy. One clear benefit was an increase in population. This was due mostly to two changes. First was the decline of the plague, which never again reached the scale of the Black Death of the fourteenth century. There were of course several explanations for this phenomenon. Partial immunity had been acquired by some segments of the population. Other reasons were social in nature and either directly or indirectly related to the increased sense of security. The end of the Hundred Years War decreased the cases of banditry and the numbers and scope of the detachments of mercenaries who were often in no way different from out-and-out criminals. For a considerable period of time there were no major wars in France, and "except for certain border provinces, little fighting took place within France between the end of the Hundred Years' War and the start of the Wars of Religion."[1] The sense of stability had positive implications for agricultural production; this certainly led to increased crop yield and an improved diet. Better-fed human bodies were more resistant to disease. It was also clear that "preventive measures taken by many towns in sixteenth century" had also contributed to the decline in the plague's impact.[2]

There were also some signs of decline of various forms of violence, for example, rape. Although rape continued to be an important part of the sexual culture, "public rapes seem to have disappeared in the course of the sixteenth century."[3] One possible explanation was that the state with comparative ease apprehended those engaged in collective rape, and punished them severely. There was also some improvement in the security of the roads, at least to the degree that it made it possible to organize a rudimentary postal courier service for the king by the sixteenth century.[4] There were also changes in mores, manifested by the slow acculturation of the French society by the end of the sixteenth century.[5] The culture of violence was still dominant. Yet the idea that violence and brutal machismo were not the only attribute of the elite started to penetrate the upper crust of society. "Francis I's court was not only larger than its predecessors; its manners were also more polished. This change is generally ascribed to the growth of Italian influence."[6] The importance of Renaissance Italy was not accidental. The new discourse, with its implication that knowledge and related manners actually differentiated the true elite from commoners, was born there. It was not accidental that Baldassare Castiglione's *Book of the Courtier*, published in 1528,[7] epitomized the beginning of the transformation of the elite from brutal, force-oriented manners to more polished, self-restricted behavior.[8]

These changes in mores were reflections of slow changes in the composition of European culture. There is no doubt that the new legalistic culture emerged with its emphasis on what was described as a "Protestant ethic." This new culture was not only the cult of work, where an earthly vocation was seen as an existential substitute for religion. It was also the culture of self-restraint and civility. These trends would in the future lead to what Durkheim described as "organic solidarity," the tightly bound, self-policed civil society of the modern West, and this would bring stability and order in the holistic meaning of the word into European society of the future.

At the same time, despite the importance of these changes, the state was not able to arrest all the most dangerous manifestations of asocial behavior, even by repression on a large scale. The state, for example, was able to diminish the scope of banditry. The armed never reached the same level as with the Hundred Years War. Yet highway banditry would not be marginalized and continued to be a serious problem. The culture of violence and the direct connection between violence with the use of weapons, mostly swords, and high social position was still popular. The distinctions in mores and behavior of the elite and lower classes in sex and other biological habits were not always clear, especially in the provinces. Consequently asocial and unsanitary behavior was quite widespread. While the Black Death never returned, the plague continued to be an important destructive force in France. To some degree it was replaced by syphilis.

Even after an additional century of continuous repression, stability and basic security would slowly penetrate only relatively small areas of the state and provide visible changes in behavior in only a small segment of the population. These positive changes would require not only the continuation of government repression but also the slow and deep transformation of society, the creation of what is called "civil society," in which behavior is self-controlled and society shares the authorities' revulsion for most manifestations of asocial behavior.

Notes

1. Knecht, *French Renaissance Monarchy*, 5.
2. Ibid.
3. Flandrin, "Repression," 32.

4.   Leon Blin, "De Lyon a Paris et Amiens: 'En diligence et en poste' (1513)," *Cahiers d'Histoire* 27, 2 (1982): 173.
5.   Robert Muchembled, "Pour une histoire des gestes, XVe-XVIIIe siècle," *Revue d'Histoire Moderne et Contemporaine* 34 (January-March 1987): 100.
6.   Knecht, *French Renaissance Monarchy*, 74.
7.   Arditi, *A Genealogy*, 4.
8.   On the importance of self restraint among the elite, see Elias, *The History*, 1: 137.

Index

Alexander III (Russia), 17
Alexandre (bastard of Bourbon), execution, 54
America, slavery 145-46
ancien régime, 25, 65, 76
Andrews, Richard, 58n13, 92n42, 93nn73,77,90, 128nn5,7,8,16
anomie, 2; fifteenth century, 52, 67; and Hobbes, 27; and Hundred Years War, 12-13
arbitrariness of punishment, 39; growth in fifteenth and sixteenth centuries, 63-65
architecture and security, 102-3
Arditi, Jorge, 92nn59,60, 160n7
Arras, brothels, 85
asocial processes: early modern Europe, 6-7, 37-38; marginal in early West, 2-3; spread of diseases, 14, 23-24
asseurement, 69
Avignon, 75, 80; edict of, 82; execution causing too much pain, 98-99

Babelon, Jean-Pierre, 96n163,176, 154n27
Ballon, Hilary Meg, 96nn160,171,175, 112n50
banditry, 67; nobles and, 11, 13-14, 51-52; armed bands, 67; priority, 38. See also mercenaries
banishment, 70-71; for sodomy in Avignon, 83
Barchilon, José, 96n166
Barkey, Karen, 30-32, 35n48, 111n22; and French failure to understand Oriental model, 32; and Ottomans, 30-31
Bauchond, Maurice, 33n10, 59n33, 93nn80,93, 95n144

Bayley, David H., 111nn21,23,12nn38,43,51
Beaune, Jacques de, 56-57
Bée, Michel, 128nn4,6,29
Bellamy, John, 21, 33nn1,33, 34n23,24, 111n20
Benabou, Erica-Marie, 95n149
Berce, Yves-Marie, 111n16, 112n49
bigamy, 82
Billaçois, François, 92nn58,59
Biraben, Jean-Noel, 96nn160,169,170, 73,180
Black Death. See plague
blasphemy, 124-25; sixteenth-century ordinances, 124; retenta to avoid, 127
Blin, Leon, 160n4
Blois, edict of (1579), 82
Boca, Jean, 59n24,27,48, 72, 92n52, 93nn93,94,94nn102,104,130,95n139, 111nn7,8, 112n32, 128nn11,33,34
Boethius, 121
Bodin, Jean, 29; ideologue of absolutist state, 29
Bosch, Hieronymus, 43
Boudriot, Pierre-Denis, 96n161
Bradford, Ernie, 154n33
Braudel, Fernand, 58nn11,12, 59nn37,45,46,50, 91n36, 111n13
Bruegel, Pieter, 43
Brezhnev, Leonid, 46
Brovkin, Vladimir, 59n43
brutality of state: essential, 23; and Machiavelli, 47; brutalization, chap. 3 passim
Bulst, Neithard, 95n155
burning, retenta, 127

capital punishment: classical times, 49; Dark and Middle Ages, 49-50;